Perspectives on American and Texas Politics

SIXTH EDITION
A Workbook for Political Science 1040

Edited by Gloria Cox

UNIVERSITY OF NORTH TEXAS

Printed in the United States of America

ISBN: 0-9741514-6-7

Eagle Images
UNIVERSITY OF NORTH TEXAS
P.O. Box 309615
Denton, Texas 76203-9615
940-565-2083

Address all correspondence and order information to the above address.

ACKNOWLEDGMENTS

The members of the faculty of the Department of Political Science sincerely hope that this manual and workbook will be an interesting and enjoyable resource for your class in American Government.

The Editor would like to express special appreciation to many people who contributed their time, expertise, and energy to the workbook, including

1. All members of the departmental faculty who wrote essays and exercises, proofread chapters, and in other ways contributed to the book;
2. Professor James Meerink who organized and directed the entire process;
3. Cece Hannah, departmental administrative assistant, for her timely and valuable assistance; and
4. Members of the University Administration for their support of this collegial endeavor.

We wish you a productive and memorable semester.

Gloria Cox, Editor

PREFACE

This workbook represents our effort as faculty members of the Department of Political Science to provide an additional resource for students of Political Science 1040 and related courses. We hope this workbook will stimulate your interest in political science, provide additional information not available in your textbook, and enhance your enjoyment of the course you are taking.

HOW TO USE THIS WORKBOOK

The subjects in this workbook parallel those you will study in Political Science 1040 at the University of North Texas. Although your professor may organize the course differently, the workbook begins with a study of the philosophical and structural foundations of American government, including liberalism, democracy, the Constitutions on the United States and Texas, and federalism. In the second section, you will have an opportunity to explore the important topics of civil liberties and civil rights. The third and final section deals with institutions of government, including the legislative, executive, administrative, and judicial branches, both at the federal and state levels. In each chapter you will find:

★ **An essay about the topic:** Each chapter contains an essay about some aspect of the topic are studying. These essays concentrate on important issues that we consider worthy of additional reading. Each essay reflects the distinctiveness of each writer's expertise and writing style and we hope that you will find them interesting, provocative, and informative.

★ **A Pro and Con piece:** We have included in each chapter a short pro and con discussion of a controversial topic. We hope that these discussions will trigger your own interest in the subject and cause you to think about it within your own political framework.

★ **Exercises:** Following each essay, you will find several exercises. Some of these exercises ask you think about and apply the concepts you have studied. Others are designed to develop your research skills and may require that you obtain information from a government textbook, the library, or the Internet. Still other exercises are check-ups on what you have learned in the chapter. Your professor may assign all of the exercises for a particular subject or only one or two. You may still wish to complete those not assigned.

We believe that you will enjoy this workbook and hope that it will add interesting material and activities to your study of political science. Best wishes for a great semester.

Gloria Cox, Editor
June 2005

TABLE OF CONTENTS

Chapter I:

The Philosophic Foundations of American Government 1

Chapter II:

Alexis de Tocqueville and American Political Culture 13

Chapter III:

The United States Constitution: Not Just for the United States Anymore? 27

Chapter IV:

The Birth of American Federalism 39

Chapter V:

Civil Liberties in the United States: Democracy and the War on Terrorism 55

Chapter VI:

An Important Issue of Civil Rights: Affirmative Action in Higher Education 71

Chapter VII:

Congress: Representation, Governance, and Legitimacy 89

Chapter VIII:

The Chief Executive 105

Chapter IX:

Problems of Control and Capture 119

Chapter X:

The Courts 133

References 155

THE PHILOSOPHIC FOUNDATIONS OF
AMERICAN GOVERNMENT
Richard S. Ruderman

That a country and its form of government should have philosophical foundations is by no means given. America was unique at the time of its founding (and remains something of a rarity today) in that it has a discernable and profound philosophical teaching that lies at the root of its existence. That teaching is called "liberalism," and it originated in the writings of such thinkers as Thomas Hobbes, Benedict Spinoza, John Locke, Baron de Montesquieu, and others in the seventeenth and eighteenth centuries. Liberalism, in its original sense, was a theory of government that was dedicated to promoting and securing liberty for its citizens. Of course, America is not and never was an exclusively liberal country. Various other movements of thought and belief—most obviously Puritanism and other religious beliefs—have played important roles in establishing the meaning of America. But liberalism has provided the framework within which these other movements have persisted and with which they have had to make their peace. That framework proudly presents itself as fundamentally "neutral," as though liberalism were the only "ism" without a political position of its own. By "neutral," we mean that liberalism purports to allow any point of view as long as it does not impose itself on others. As we shall see, liberalism is in fact "neutral" only provisionally or as a tactic: like every other "ism," it does advance (if somewhat indirectly and hence obscurely) a political agenda of its own. In order to understand both the stated and the implicit agendas of liberalism, we must return to the thinkers who were its architects. We who are its beneficiaries are apt to take for granted certain outlooks and views that were looked on with suspicion, if not hostility, at the start. Moreover, liberalism is peculiar in that it encourages a certain kind of forgetfulness about its origins (contrary, for instance, to many religions, which demand a constant looking back at their origins). Its founders can explain why.

Before returning to them, however, it is worth taking stock of liberalism's current stature at home and in the world. In the United States, the meaning of liberalism has morphed considerably since its inception. At its origin, the United States was proud to call itself the world's first liberal democracy. There had been democracies before (most famously in ancient Athens) but never a *liberal* democracy, one based on what Publius called (in *Federalist Paper #9*) the new "science of politics." Its advances included the separation of powers, checks and balances, independent courts, representation, and the "enlargement of the orbit" or the size of the country. Liberalism begins from the following premises: people are individuals before they are citizens or members of any group (social, economic or religious) and hence must choose or *consent to* any associations they may join; people are at bottom self-interested and cannot be blamed for being so; people are rational (more or less) in their ability to grasp and secure that self-interest; and government is needed to secure our rights (from other wicked individuals, from our own collective acts of self-indulgence or irresponsibility and, last but not least, from government itself). For these and related reasons, liberalism could originally be characterized as a sober philosophy devoted to the free accumulation of property and to the development of the bourgeois virtues (thrift, self-reliance, disapproval of self-expression, etc.) associated with it. Many, if not most, Democrats and Republicans, as well as most so-called "liberals" and "conservatives," are then "liberals" in this sense (even if they differ over the most important sphere—say, economic or sexual—in which to secure liberty).

As liberalism took hold, however, it came to be impatient with what Winston Churchill called its "low but solid" materialistic outlook. Above all, it wished to shift from its original negative goal (of holding sickness, poverty, and death at bay) to a positive one of "autonomy" or the development of a unique, unrepressed personality. The bourgeois virtues on which liberal democracy had heretofore rested came to be seen as obstacles to this development and were replaced, over time, with a taste for eccentricity, for progressive—and costly—politics, for irrationality in various guises (Freud's subconscious, "primitivism" in music and art, Romanticism in literature, existentialism, etc.)

and finally, in our day, by a dedication to diversity. In short, an outlook that was in many ways "conservative" became "liberal" in its present sense. We are thus presented with the odd fact that calling someone a "liberal" in an American political ad has become damaging and that, in some European countries, conservatives are called "liberal" and liberals are called "progressive."

In order to grasp this evolution, it is worth focusing for a moment on the fact that liberalism, initially presented as a philosophy for the liberation of all, can today be seen as one in which the elites are most at home. Actually, liberalism was initially a kind of alliance between philosophers and the common man against the powers of the old "elite" of the aristocracy, the monarchy, and the Church. In exchange for freedom of inquiry (and freedom from the persecution that had plagued them since the time of Socrates), philosophers offered, via the twin pillars of toleration and applied science (or technology), to supply humanity at large with comfortable self-preservation. This would entail putting an end to what Machiavelli called the "ambitious idleness" of aristocrats and priests (*Discourses on Livy*, Book I, Preface). That is, liberalism sought to delegitimate the authority of those who ruled chiefly through the spending of unearned wealth (acquired through inheritance or collecting tithes from others). It would transfer that authority from the "Quarrelsom and Contentious" to the "Industrious and Rational" (Locke, *Two Treatises of Government*, 2.34). The unproductive classes—be they contemplative dreamers, fox-hunting aristocrats, or otherworldly priests reliant on taxes and on governments willing to "establish" religion on their behalf—must make way for the hard-working common man.

Yet, a closer look at these Lockean categories reveals some oddities. Who precisely are the "Quarrelsom and Contentious," on the one hand, and the "Industrious and Rational," on the other? The former turn out to be those who take morality—and in particular justice—seriously. Because they take it seriously—and because the precise meaning of justice is inherently complex and elusive—morally serious people are apt to disagree and to dispute among themselves. Older philosophers were not troubled by this outlook and, in fact, welcomed it—witness Socrates' endless engagements in "dialectic," reasoned

disputation bent on discovering the needed truth about justice. They would, in fact, have labeled as "rational" *only* those who contended so over the meaning of justice, convinced that "the unexamined life is not worth living." On what grounds, then, does Locke instead label as "rational" those who have put aside or outgrown the need for moral disputation? Locke's connection of the rational with the industrious provides the clue. Those who concentrate on matters of the soul (its proper ordering, its fulfillment, its alleged capacity to transcend itself and its temporal environment) are, in Locke's view, chasing a will-o'-the-wisp and are thereby condemned to endless and pointless quarrels and disputes. As Gertrude Stein famously said of Oakland: "there's no 'there' there." But those who concentrate on the body and its far more clear and distinct needs can come to terms. Protecting the body in all its vulnerability from hunger, illness, poverty, and death can put "abstract" moral disputes into the shade and replace them with scientific and economic questions of the efficient management of resources and the orderly administration of things.

It was left to John Stuart Mill (1806-1873) to reevaluate the partnership between thinkers and the "many" after the fall of the old elites. By the mid-nineteenth century, it was becoming more and more apparent that the old authorities of the Church and the Monarchy would soon be no more. In fact, the German philosopher Friedrich Nietzsche would soon make his infamous pronouncement that "God is dead" by which he meant that all higher ideals or principles had lost their legitimacy and hence their power over our hearts and minds. In this atmosphere, Mill determined that lazy conformism to the unadventurous mental life of the middle class had replaced oppression by any higher classes as the chief threat to human liberty. In a fateful choice, he promoted "diversity" and "individualism" as liberalism's new ideals, anxiously hoping that the "geniuses" who would thereby prosper would in turn benefit the public at large—even though the latter would likely find offensive many of the "experiments in living" carried out by the former (and their freethinker imitators). Thus began the strain between the freethinking elites and the culturally conservative citizens at large that continues to bedevil liberalism even today. It is almost as if, in the words of Mary Ann Glendon, we have become a nation of "Yahoos" and "perverts": to the intellectual elite, most of "Middle America" seems populated by unsophisticated Yahoos who still go to church and denounce some behavior as "immoral" while, to Middle America, most of the cultural, artistic, and academic leaders appear to be perverts whose various modes of self-indulgence are never checked by responsibility to social standards, much less by patriotism.

Outside of America (or the West), liberalism (in both its original and its present senses) has run up against mounting and even ferocious opposition. Condemned for its materialistic devotion to work, money, and possessions as well as for its unrestrained self-expression that is often viewed as immoral, American liberalism finds itself increasingly hard-pressed to define, defend, or promote itself as Lincoln's "last, best hope on Earth." That many people today firmly resist liberalism's offer of liberation has been something of a shock to Americans. They had always held that people the world over were the same, once you scratched the surface of their wildly disparate seeming cultures. They wanted to be free to choose their own careers, spouses, pastimes, and religions. One might even say that the historical development of liberalism was *designed* to function as a seductive call that would attract people from all the various pre-liberal or illiberal cultures to its demonstrable capacity to provide a life of "comfortable self-preservation." Why, then, would Iran (which was, in 1979, perhaps the most rapidly modernizing country outside of the West) reject liberalism and, instead, embrace fundamentalist Islam? Why would the sons of aspiring middle-class parents, many of whom had visited and even studied in the West, and not simply poor or ignorant people, join Osama bin Laden to strike at America on September 11th? In brief, why would anyone consciously *return* to religious authoritarianism after seeing what liberalism had to offer?

In order to understand both liberalism's expectations and the meaning of the largely fundamentalist rejection of liberalism, we must study the origin, scope, and purpose of liberalism. The first liberal was arguably Thomas Hobbes (1588-1679). We can say this despite the fact that Hobbes never used the term "liberalism" and despite the even more glaring fact that Hobbes promoted absolute monarchy as the best form of government. Hobbes wanted a government that was as limited in its aims as it was unlimited in its power to achieve them. It was through his discovery and promotion of *limited* government— of a government that, however unchecked it was in the public sphere, would nevertheless leave citizens more or less alone in the newly discovered private sphere of "civil society"—that Hobbes secured the first steps of liberalism. Earlier forms of government—whether the republicanism that traced its roots back to Aristotle's suggestion that government should make people "doers of noble deeds" or the various divine governments intent on chastening and even purifying their citizens' souls—did not hesitate to intervene in the innermost lives of citizens. Using civil (parochial) or revealed (universal) religion, invasive and demanding moral education, and censorship designed to capture the hearts and minds of the citizens for the regime, these earlier governments asserted or assumed that everything was potentially its business. Hobbes's government, by contrast, would never demand any form of transcendence on the part of its citizens. They would be free, in fact, to remain largely as fearful, calculating, and self-regarding as they had been in the State of Nature (prior to the existence of any government). Above all, they would be free (as most modern Americans are) to be utterly apolitical. It was Hobbes's contention that only vain opinion-mongers (potential leaders) and poor, ignorant people unaware that worldly comforts were within their grasp and could satisfy their longings (potential followers) were interested in politics. Private life, if protected from manipulative leaders and from moral busybodies demanding that we attend to the lives of our fellow citizens, could be wholly fulfilling. Thus, Hobbes's famous inversion of the Golden Rule: "do not do unto Others as you would not have them do onto you." Rather than actively seeking to *do* unto others (which, Hobbes implied, always ended up requiring you to do something *to* others, such as the Spanish Inquisition did), Hobbes would have us simply leave one another alone.

Still, Hobbes insisted that only an absolute sovereign would have the requisite strength to maintain the peace that would function as the basis of a safe, secure, and productive society. It was left to John Locke (1632-1704), the father of liberalism in the strict sense, to ensure that the government that secured our freedom from one another's wicked or designing schemes did not itself then turn around and threaten that very liberty. He therefore devised the famous "separation of powers" (to use government's power against itself) as well as the right to revolution (to encourage citizens to be vigilant *against government* in the defense of liberty). Above all, Locke attempted to show us the meaning of the truly rational private life: the unlimited pursuit of property. For property, properly understood, could solve the age-old dilemma of how to divide up the pie. It was because people feared that they would receive a too-small slice of a finite pie that they were prompted to establish standards of "justice" by which to stake their claim to a larger slice. And most of these standards of justice came down hard on "greed," the readiness to possess more than your fair share. But, as Locke demonstrates, the taking of property for the purpose of developing it through one's *labor* would actually increase rather than decrease the overall size of the pie. Labor contributes perhaps 99.99% of the value of things. This has two notable effects: (1) people anxious about the prospect of not having enough to make ends meet could now set about directly remedying their situation by accumulating more property rather than indirectly (and somewhat disingenuously) trying to show that "justice" demanded that they be given such-and-such a share, and (2) the desire to "have more" could be divided into the unacceptable desire to have what belongs to others and the more-than-acceptable desire to strike it rich by using one's labor (intellectual as well as physical) to generate more of one's own.

The importance of Locke's new understanding of property and its place in the overall political economy of government cannot be overstated. It meant that "unused" (that is to say, undeveloped) land could no longer be morally defended. This struck a blow at the heart of aristocratic government, which had always been based on the landed aristocracy. The great French observer of American democracy, Alexis de Tocqueville, said that nothing would have a more profound democratizing effect on a society than to replace the law of primogeniture (requiring that aristocrats deed their entire, undivided estates to their oldest male children) with a law of inheritance that allows them to divide up their estates and deed them to whomsoever they will. Land becomes "real estate," and a once static

economy becomes a very dynamic one. Family ties that had given fathers (not mothers) an almost "supernatural" hold over their family's future would be sundered, leaving each generation free to rise (or fall) on its own. Hard work and the readiness to treat everything as fair game for economic activity became the new order of the day. Leisure, once the basis for higher human accomplishments (chiefly art and philosophy), even came to be suspect as "unproductive."

Lest this extremely self-regarding, not to say selfish, line of argument overwhelm us, it is important not to overlook the moral side of Lockean liberalism. While most of the old moral demands (against greed, for obedience to parents, for a zealous dedication to justice, etc.) fell by the wayside, one new moral demand arose to replace them: toleration. (One of Locke's most important writings is his *Letter Concerning Toleration*.) Though it has become second nature to us, toleration is, from the point of view of the old morality, a most peculiar outlook. In fact, it can appear to be an inversion of morality. Just as the old morality demanded that we take seriously, in large part by imposing, the requirements of justice, toleration demands that we show our dedication to justice by overcoming, or at least restraining, this tendency. Thus, where pre-Lockean preachers in America were wont to say that "we certainly cannot tolerate sin, vice, and the adversaries of God's Truth," post-Lockean preachers urged us to tolerate each man's right to his opinion.

Toleration was initially promoted as being good for both society and religion. Society, heretofore rent (especially in Europe) by religious warfare, could begin to adopt a "live and let live" attitude. And religion, apt in the past to bring out the cruel and hypocritical sides in its adherents, would henceforth stop imposing itself on people and instead would await their sincere interest and acceptance. Yet, according to liberalism's most profound teachers, toleration would also have a subterranean, slow-acting influence on the character of religious belief. To be more precise, toleration was counted on by these thinkers to weaken the power of religion more than any frontal, repressive assault ever could. In fact, how could it not? Religion, after all, was being asked to convert itself from "the Way and the Truth" to a mere opinion or, rather, to a gaggle of opinions. Above all, it was being asked to transform itself from a controlling truth imposed on us from without to a chosen (or rejected) opinion generated from within. The early liberal philosophers wagered that personal choice, always able to reconsider itself at some future date, would never rise to the level of harsh, unbending finality enjoyed by externally imposed Divine obligations. In particular, they assumed that the pressing cares of attaining and assuring a comfortable self-preservation would, of themselves, tempt individuals to think less and less—and thus be moved less and less—by religious considerations. Thus, Montesquieu observed:

> It is not ... by filling the soul with [fear of one's own death] ... that one succeeds in detaching the soul from religion; a more certain way to attack religion is by favor, by the comforts of life, by the hope of fortune; not by what reminds one of [death] but by what makes one forget it; not by what makes one indignant but by what casts one into indifference when other passions act on our souls and when those that religion inspires are silent. General rule: in the matter of changing religion, invitations are stronger than penalties (*The Spirit of the Laws*, 25.12).

Toleration, that is, by letting people devote themselves to what they will, supplements the newfound dedication to property with the result that the religious impulse will weaken and wither over time.

In America, Jefferson was perhaps the most acute student of these softening effects of toleration. Following Montesquieu, he presented himself as indifferent to religious opinions ("it does me no injury for my neighbor to say that there are twenty gods or no gods") and applauded those states that had made the "happy discovery" that "the way to silence religious disputes, is to take no notice of them." But did this bold experiment, masquerading as humility before insoluble transcendental riddles, succeed? Or has America remained exceptional in religious observance, as in so many other things, when compared to other modern nations, in particular European ones? According to Henry Adams, despite the ongoing rituals and continuous church attendance still in evidence in America, "the religious instinct had vanished" sometime during the nineteenth century. It was, he wrote, "the most curious phenomenon he had to account for in a long life."

Liberalism, in sum, sought to satisfy humanity—potentially *all* of humanity—by focusing on its real, bodily needs. Treating the old moral demands as distractions from, if not obstacles to, the necessary business of conquering Nature for the purpose (in the words of Francis Bacon) of "relieving Man's estate," liberalism sought to defuse the disputes and even wars produced by those moral demands by appearing to evade them.

Adopting a "neutral" stance, and encouraging a tolerant, indifferent attitude among the populace at large, liberalism expected to offer such astonishing material rewards to its very busy followers that they would, over time, simply forget about the exacting religious demands that would come to seem irrelevant to the pursuit of happiness. More than any other political theory, then, liberalism would have to be proved true in deed rather than in abstract debate. If people truly embraced life under liberalism and if they no longer felt the kinds of dissatisfactions that (according to the liberal analysis) prompted them to seek "spiritual" satisfactions of various kinds, liberalism would be vindicated. As a result, liberals continue to insist (as per their theory) that poverty and hopelessness alone breed revolutionaries, suicide bombers, and fundamentalists. For, if (as it appears) upwardly mobile, educated, semi-Westernized individuals from illiberal lands *also* begin to reject and even hate liberalism, we may be witnessing the undermining of liberalism's initial promise and strategy. Perhaps, then, America's greater supply of non-liberal characteristics (especially when compared to Europe) will stand it in good stead.

PRO & CON
Is Liberalism A Moral and Political Philosophy That Speaks To All People?

One of the most powerful documents of liberalism is the American Declaration of Independence (1776). It speaks, among other things, of the "self-evident truths" that "all men are created equal," that all men have rights to "life, liberty, and the pursuit of happiness," and that "governments are instituted to secure these rights." These phrases imply that *every* individual (male, female, black, white, rich, poor, Christian, Muslim, pagan, etc.) can recognize or discover the teachings of liberalism—no revelation, no class status, and no peculiarly gendered mind is required to understand them. Furthermore, they imply that the teachings of liberalism *apply* to every individual, whether or not they have yet been liberated. Every individual would, given a modicum of enlightenment and half a chance to speak freely, eagerly embrace the chance to live under a regime of rights and a government devoted to securing them. Thus, it is not right to speak of American "cultural imperialism": American-style liberal democracy keeps spreading simply because people want it as soon as it becomes available to them, as John Locke predicted.

YES! Diversity is a distraction. However kaleidoscopic the world's cultures may seem, underneath them all one finds simple human beings. And human beings are, at bottom, the same. Because of their undisciplined imaginations, humans have, throughout our history, been all too apt to follow charismatic leaders who promise them such things as "cultural identity" or even some form of "cultural uniqueness" or "superiority." These tempting dreams now stand revealed as "ethnocentrism," that is, as comforting (or dangerous) delusions that have no basis in reality. The needs of all peoples, whatever their strutting cultural or political spokespeople say, are essentially the same: food, shelter, health, creature comforts, and bodily satisfactions. True, there are various cultures that deny this. These cultures still insist that people need morality above all: clear and demanding guidelines for personal behavior including sexual behavior, military courage, and the overcoming of greed or selfishness. Liberalism has taught us, however, that such demands amount to little more than pointless repression. It is both unnecessary and impossible to overcome the natural human preference for oneself and one's own satisfactions. It is unnecessary because the widespread acceptance of the Lockean pursuit of property will relieve more of humanity's ills than charity and self-denial ever did. And, because it is impossible (self-interest will always out in the end), asking us to live up to such moral standards will breed nothing but hypocrites and imposters. It is better to admit, with Gordon Gekko of the movie *Wall Street*, that "greed is good." The hope for personal monetary gain is the engine that will drive humanity to ever-higher levels of comfort and freedom. And by ending the stigma that was always attached to it in the past, we can even enjoy our wealth (and all the health and pleasures it can buy) with a clear conscience. Above all, we may assume that only the poor and dispossessed (both at home and abroad) harbor the dissatisfaction that breeds crime, resentment, and terrorist ambitions. Raise their standard of living, give them "new economy" skills, and offer them a multicultural education, and they will surely learn to tolerate others, to relax (and maybe even drop) their inflexible morals, and to devote themselves to the mutually beneficial business of the global economy.

Moreover, toleration is good not only for society and for those previously discriminated against; but also for the tolerant themselves. By tolerating other cultures and peoples, we open ourselves up to learning about them and perhaps even to admiring them. And by thus widening our circle of life-choices, we free ourselves from the fate of living mere copies of the lives handed to us by our culture, our religion, or our parents. Toleration is the necessary basis for autonomy and for freely choosing the components of a unique way of life that is truly mine.

NO! Liberalism's promise to tolerate all ways of life in a "neutral" or even-handed fashion is a false one. In order to live under liberalism, one (or one's children) must become in fact "liberal." While this step will provide great material comforts, it will come at a cost. Parents will lose all meaningful authority over their children (and situation comedies on TV will vigorously promote this change); individuals who were once citizens or aristocratic leaders or lazy dreamers or political intriguers will all become consumers and producers; and all the signs of human dignity—refined speech, modest clothing, restrained sexual behavior— will be overwhelmed by the ever narrower and more specialized demands of the job market and by "mass culture," invariably crass and vulgar, if also fun and distracting. Moreover, we cannot forget that promoting liberty tends to undermine both equality and community. Leaving people free to pursue property means that some—the hardworking, the inspired, and the lucky—will amass far more of it than others. Liberalism may *permit* the poor to become rich; however, it will surely do little to erase the distinction of rich and poor. Thus, exploitation by the rich will continue and crime, desperation, and hopelessness will continue to be the fate of the poor. But this is really the least of liberalism's problems. By emphasizing individualism, liberalism ensures that a suspicious, self-protective attitude will pervade the citizenry. Taught by bestsellers (if not by life itself) to "look out for #1," liberal citizens will become incapable of truly devoting themselves to others. Yes, they may "understand" them, but, having been taught that all cultures are equal, they cannot look up to them. Treating a foreign culture as a mere resource for my individual choice, moreover, fatally misrepresents the culture, for all other (illiberal) cultures do not recognize individualism. They expect the individual to take his or her pre-assigned place within that culture.

Turning back home, we will find that self-regarding individuals cannot become really good friends, spouses, citizens, or parents. After all, each of these relations involves something of an imposition on my "private space." However much I may enjoy certain aspects of these relations, I will eventually come to a point where I resent their demands on me. If I consent to all these relations only insofar as I expect them to contribute to my happiness, why should I make any sacrifices to them at the cost of my happiness? This is the gravest ill of liberalism: we come to feel a fundamental sense of alienation from others, a punishing sense that we must do everything for ourselves with little or no guidance from our culture, and a sense of loneliness or isolation even in the midst of the busy "rat race" to which we all seem to be condemned. We long for "community" but, having become individual "choosers" who always reserve the right to reconsider our options, we cannot take the necessary plunge into any particular community. Perhaps, as John Stuart Mill said, liberalism can satisfy those few "geniuses" among us, those happy to be cosmopolitan wanderers throughout the various cultures of the world, picking and choosing what interests us from among them but, in the end, giving our hearts to none of them. As for the rest of us who wish to live lives that aren't wholly consumed by hectic work and escapist entertainment, who want to live within a culture and not to observe it from the outside, we will have to look to cultures other than the liberal one.

EXERCISE 1-1
Thinking About American Individualism

Some nations, including France and Japan, have Citizen Assist Laws (so-called Good Samaritan laws) whereby people can be punished (usually with a fine) for failing to come to the assistance of someone in need. In the United States, where the philosophy of individualism is stronger, courts have consistently held that even if you see someone bleeding to death on the road and you have bandages in your car, you can't be punished for ignoring that person and driving by.

Occasionally, the debate over this issue is revived by some particularly horrendous case of someone ignoring the needs of another. One incident involved a teenage male who walked away and did nothing when he witnessed his friend engaged in the sexual assault and murder of a ten-year-old girl. Another case involved the gang rape of a teenage girl by several men while other men looked on without intervening to stop the attack. Cases like these have caused many Americans to consider whether we have more responsibility to one another than incidents like these two would indicate.

In a news story from June 2005, a man was called a Good Samaritan when he interrupted a crime. He was passing by a residence when he heard sounds of struggle as a young man slashed his girlfriend and her mother with a knife. The passerby went into the home, subdued the assailant, and held him until police arrived. (Story retrieved from the Internet on June 30, 2005.) In another news item from the same week, the life of a young man was saved after he suffered a shark attack in the Gulf of Mexico when vacationing doctors and nurses came to his aid until an ambulance arrived.

On a separate sheet of paper, in a brief essay of at least ten sentences, use one or more of the examples above to 1) explain why you think that we need or do not need laws to require that one person come to the aid of another in emergency situations, and 2) discuss the impact of your view on the American value of individualism.

EXERCISE 1-2
Thinking About the Pro & Con

After reading the foregoing "Pro & Con" section, write an essay in the space provided below in which you defend the side that you find most persuasive. Give specific examples from life stories that you are directly familiar with or that you have read about in books, magazines, newspapers, etc. Above all, consider "clashes" between the liberal outlook and that of non-liberal cultures.

_____

_____

_____

_____

_____

_____

_____

_____

_____

_____

_____

_____

_____

Name	Seat	Score

EXERCISE 1-3
American Differences

As mentioned in the essay, Mary Ann Glendon (in her book *Rights Talk*) writes that sometimes it seems that America is divided into "Yahoos" and "perverts." By this she means that the intellectual/academic/artistic/political elite tends to look at Middle America and see culturally unsophisticated "Yahoos" who are uncomfortable with "obscene" art, who strongly oppose adultery or "alternate lifestyles," and who still seek guidance and comfort in the Bible. At the same time, Middle America tends to view dwellers in the big cities on the coasts and the leaders of intellectual and artistic life in America as "perverts" whose self-indulgent lifestyles make a mockery out of American (or Judeo-Christian) values.

Consider any recent public dispute—over government funding for the arts or National Public Radio, over attitudes to foreigners, over religious influence in the schools (e.g., creationism or internet filters on school library computers), etc.—and explain the basis for the mutual misunderstandings that are involved. In a one-page essay, try to explain which side in the dispute can be said to speak for the "classical liberal" outlook.

_____

_____

_____

_____

_____

_____

_____

_____

_____

_____

_____

_____

Name		Seat	Score

ALEXIS DE TOCQUEVILLE
AND AMERICAN POLITICAL CULTURE
Steven Forde

In the 1830s, a French aristocrat named Alexis de Tocqueville traveled extensively in the United States, making observations about American democracy. In 1835 and 1840, he published two volumes of a work, *Democracy in America*, that is widely read to this day. One of Tocqueville's claims is that American politics cannot be explained solely on the basis of the country's laws and constitutions. Of equal importance are Americans' beliefs, attitudes, and mores.

These factors generally go under the name of "political culture" today, and their importance is immense. For example, Americans are more individualistic than citizens in many other democracies and have a much more suspicious attitude toward government in general. This helps explain why there is relatively less government regulation and less redistribution of wealth here than in many other countries. Americans also tend to have negative attitudes toward politics and politicians and to be somewhat uninformed and apathetic when it comes to politics. If these are your attitudes, you are a typical product of American political culture.

In Tocqueville's day, democracy was a novel form of government. The United States was the only working democracy of any size in the world. Democracy had failed, or was struggling, in other countries; Tocqueville was trying to figure out what made it work in America. His question was the same one people ask today: why does democracy work in some places and not in others? Why is it not enough for a nation simply to adopt a democratic constitution and laws? One reason is that democracy requires a certain type of political culture to be successful, and developing a new culture is much more difficult than adopting a new constitution. *Democracy in America* is a detailed and insightful analysis of the cultural attitudes and institutions that Tocqueville believed to be key to healthy democracy in America. But, while he admired American political culture, he also found some flaws and hidden dangers that might threaten the health of American democracy in the future. We will look at just a few of his key insights. If you want to learn more, it is easy to browse through *Democracy in America* on your own.

Learning Citizenship

Democracy places greater faith in the people than other forms of government, but it also places greater burdens on them. A certain level of citizen engagement is necessary to the health of any democratic system. Voters must gain information on political issues and evaluate that information before they vote. They must pay enough attention to politics to call government to account when it oversteps its bounds. This burden is lessened by representation, which entrusts actual policy decisions to elected representatives, and by checks and balances, which has the representatives check each other. But, a certain amount of grassroots civic responsibility is still required. Citizens must be willing to devote some time and effort to the common good, not just their private good.

Tocqueville said that the American system of the 1830s fostered good citizenship partly through the institution of local self-government. American townships were vibrant, self-governing entities, and it was here that Americans learned the skills of democracy. Participation in town hall meetings and other local institutions gave Americans hands-on experience in the workings of government. This showed them how the system works and how they could make the system work for them. In addition, local participation taught them about the compromises and trade-offs that are unavoidable in politics, and that you win sometimes and you lose sometimes. Above all, it taught them how to take responsibility for the affairs of their community. Local self-government in America, said Tocqueville, was the "primary school" of American democracy.

These skills were further sharpened by the American propensity to form political associations. In a democracy, citizens individually have a very limited capacity to change things. To be effective, they have to learn how to combine forces. Tocqueville was amazed at the American ability to band together for political causes. There were neighborhood associations, temperance unions, and clubs devoted to conservation, to the abolition of slavery, or even to the repair of local roads. When Americans identified a problem, said Tocqueville, they didn't wait for government to solve it but in ad formed an association to address it. The tiative, the organizational skills, and the prot m-solving attitude Americans developed this ay contributed immensely to their effectiveness a emocratic citizens.

Tocquevi contrasts American citizens with the commo people found in the European countries of s day. If a public road is blocked in a rural villa there, he says, it never even occurs to the peo that they can do anything about it. They passi ly wait for someone from the central governme to come and fix the problem for them. In American township, by contrast, a local co mittee is immediately formed, the problem surveyed, equipment and personnel are rounde p, and the problem is solved, unless it is absolut / beyond local capacities. This may result in ha zard and inconsistent problem–solving acros he nation, but the real benefit of this syste according to Tocqueville, is that it shapes Ame ans into active, responsible citizens. It wou be much more difficult to construct a suc ssful democracy with the European peasants he scribes than with these Americans.

American democracy is healthy partly because c ne initiative citizens develop at the local level. Tocqueville warned that local self-government a fragile thing. If the central government were take too many functions out of local hands, this primary school of democracy" could easily ither. No one will get involved in local politics if no important decisions are made locally. Americans might then sink into the kind of passivity Tocqueville observed in the Europeans of his day, and American democracy would be weakened. The same would happen if Americans got out of the habit of forming and joining political associations.

In a democracy, Tocqueville says, there is a natural but dangerous tendency to what he calls "individualism." Tocqueville defines individualism as people withdrawing from public life and public concerns. They essentially abdicate their citizenship, devoting themselves only to their private lives, to their jobs, and to the small circle of their family and friends. This may seem harmless enough, but if an active citizenry were necessary for healthy democracy, this kind of individualism would actually endanger democracy. "Individualists" are apathetic about public business, and would rather just leave it to others. This tendency is natural in democracy because

each individual has very little effect on the political system by himself, and there is a natural tendency to get wrapped up in your own concerns and let public affairs take care of themselves. In a democracy people have a right to do this, obviously, but if it becomes widespread, democracy will be in jeopardy.

Democracy and Religion

One of Tocqueville's most remarkable claims about American democracy is that religion plays a key role in its success. He says that religion needs to be considered the first of the Americans' political institutions. And yet the Americans, unlike many European nations of the time, have no established religion. In fact, their whole system is based on a separation of church and state. How can this be?

Tocqueville begins by arguing that key parts of a nation's political culture are formed at the nation's birth. In this case, the birth is 1620, when the Pilgrims landed in the New World. The Pilgrims were Puritans, members of a very strict Christian denomination, and their religious attitudes shaped their political culture. For example, they had a very strong sense of the difference between "liberty" and "license." Liberty is fine, but it must be exercised responsibly. License is the abuse of liberty. You have a right to throw a party, but not to keep the whole neighborhood awake with it. The strict moral code of the Puritans, according to Tocqueville, prevented them from abusing their liberty.

A system of government in which citizens have a great deal of freedom paradoxically requires a stronger moral code among the citizenry than other forms of government: People can't safely be given liberty unless you can trust them not to abuse it. They must respect the rights of others and they must have self-restraint. These things come from morality. This is why religion is more necessary to democracy than any other form of government. Religion is the most powerful force for morality in most people's lives. The Puritans of 1620 were long gone, but Tocqueville claimed that two hundred years after, in his day, American political culture was still shaped by religious morality—and that was a good thing. It was a hidden key to the success of American democracy.

Religion has other hidden benefits as well. Democracy is based on open debate and discussion of all public issues. It is restless, innovative, and always open to new ideas and experiments. This attitude is fine in the political arena, but it is dangerous if pushed too far. If people start to call into question the fundamental moral principles on which all of society is based, this innovative spirit can become risky. Tocqueville found it remarkable that the Americans were so freewheeling in their political debates where literally nothing was sacred, but when it came to religion and basic moral principles, no one even thought of questioning them. In some European societies, doctrines like atheism and anarchism circulated freely, and people openly advocated violence as a political tool. The religiously based moral code of the Americans prevented anyone from even imagining such things, according to Tocqueville. In our day, ideologies like fascism and communism, together with ideas like slavery, are considered morally abhorrent by Americans, and they are effectively shut out of the political system. Without the government having to censor speech or ideas, American democracy is protected from some potentially dangerous ideas, and Tocqueville attributes this partly to the nation's religious heritage.

Two things must be mentioned here so that we don't misunderstand Tocqueville's point. First, his argument about the importance of religion to democracy has nothing to do with the truth of religion. From a political point of view, the truth of people's religious beliefs is less important than the fact that religious belief makes them moral. Belief in Zeus would be as good as any other faith if it made people moral. From a political point of view, Tocqueville says that it does not matter what people's religion is, so long as they *have* one. In his view, even atheists who understand politics will realize this, and will publicly support the cause of religion just because healthy democracy requires it.

Second, the political importance of religion in democracy does not mean that a democracy should set up an official religion or an established church. In fact, Tocqueville claims religion is much better situated to perform its political role if it is separated from the state, as in America. Since the political job of religion is to safeguard a realm of moral truths that are off limits to political debate, a realm of moral certainty *outside* of politics, it is actually better that religion not be directly involved in politics. Tocqueville noted that the American preachers of his day deliberately stayed out of politics and tended not even to take

sides on political issues. To get involved in politics would only discredit them. They would no longer be seen as keepers of absolute moral truth but as political partisans, and their usefulness to democracy would be lessened.

The "Tyranny of the Majority"

Tyranny is an age-old political problem. For millennia, monarchies or aristocracies were almost the only form of government, and they often abused their power. But now that democracy has been established in more and more countries, that problem has been solved. With the people ruling themselves, tyranny is a thing of the past.

At least, that was the view of many advocates of democracy. Unfortunately, it turned out not to be true. Democracy is not really rule by the whole people over themselves, but rule of the majority over themselves and the minority. And the majority, being human, can abuse its power just as well as any monarch or aristocrat. In some respects, the problem might be worse. Under an oppressive monarch, you could at least seek refuge in aristocratic or popular support, but in a democracy, there is literally nowhere to turn for support against a tyrannical majority. Minorities might be in greater jeopardy in a democracy than under any other government.

Intelligent advocates of democracy always understood this problem. James Madison, in *Federalist #10,* describes the problem as "majority faction" and shows how the American Constitutional system combats it. Tocqueville called this problem the "tyranny of the majority," and agreed that, in the political arena, American democracy had fairly effective safeguards against it. The constitutional checks and balances, plus the American knack for organizing into associations when necessary to resist the majority, mostly contained the problem. But there were other aspects of majority tyranny that it had dealt with less effectively.

Democracy prides itself on fostering a robust individualism where people can do or say almost anything they want. But Tocqueville was surprised to find, when he arrived in America, that true individualism was rare. Americans were officially at liberty to do as they pleased, yet everyone dressed the same, everyone talked the same, and everyone had essentially the same tastes and the same ideas. There was more real diversity in old monarchical and aristocratic Europe. Instead of individualism, America seemed to cultivate conformity. Tocqueville went so far as to say that "there is less independence of mind and true freedom of discussion" in America than in almost any other country.

What could explain this? Tocqueville blames it on a form of the "tyranny of the majority" whereby the majority controls not just politics but culture and thought as well. In a democracy, the pressure to conform to the majority in everything is too strong for individuals to resist. In essence, they succumb to a kind of majority peer pressure. If the majority has not made up its mind on an issue, says Tocqueville, people do as they please, but when the majority decides, everyone scrambles to get on the bandwagon. The pressure to conform is so strong partly because democracy, based on majority rule, creates a presumption in everyone's mind that the majority must be right. This presumption extends beyond politics to culture generally. And so, when individuals are looking around, trying to figure out how to dress or what to think, they naturally, and almost subconsciously, follow the lead of the majority. They follow prevailing taste or fashion, which is the taste and fashion of the majority.

Beyond that, Tocqueville argues democratic individuals conform because they are inherently weak. Collectively, democratic individuals are strong, but individually, they are weak. In a sense, we have the individualism of particles of dust. Each particle is too weak to resist the pressure to conform when a majority of the others has decided something. Tocqueville contrasts our situation with the situation of aristocrats in the old European system. By birth, an aristocrat occupied a position of leadership in society, above the common level. He was raised from birth to think of himself that way, and everyone around him treated him that way. Such a person would be more likely to have the confidence to blaze a new trail: it was not for him to conform to what others think but for others to conform to him. This is the kind of confidence or inner strength that democratic individuals lack, making them vulnerable to the tyranny of the majority not just in politics but in everything.

This is obviously a problem for democratic cultures, but Tocqueville points out that it has some positive uses too. In the last section, we saw how the ironclad moral beliefs of Americans prevent some dangerous ideas from gaining

ground. This, in Tocqueville's mind, is a positive use of majority tyranny. But, he warns that this power can also stifle good things. Majority tyranny is almost built into the nature of democracy, and it is something that democratic citizens and legislators have to be worried about.

Equality and its Problems

Tocqueville said the most important single characteristic of American society was its absolute equality of conditions. The Americans of his day tended not to recognize this—they were more likely to get irritated at the fact that some were rich and others were poor. But for Tocqueville, this only proved his point: in a time when European societies still had aristocrats with inherited political privileges, where poor people often could not vote and had many career paths closed to them, the American notion that their society was unequal only showed that they didn't even know what true inequality was. Inequalities of wealth existed, of course, but the *principle* of equality was so firmly rooted that it had the status of one of those sacred moral truths that no one even dared to question. Every politician and every wealthy person, no matter how rich or exalted, pledged allegiance to the principle of equality— and they *meant* it. No one anywhere in America believed that riches or elected office made you "better" than anyone else or entitled you to any special rights.

According to Tocqueville, Americans are justified in celebrating equality. An egalitarian society really is more just than a society of inherited privilege. It gives the common man dignity and allows him to develop mental and other faculties. By providing opportunity for all, equality produces a very dynamic and prosperous society. However, the political culture of equality also has some negative effects of which Tocqueville says we must be aware. One of them is irritation at perceived violations of equality, even if they are unavoidable or justified. In a culture devoted to equality, there is a tendency to demand not only equality of opportunity, but also equality of result. One of the greatest dangers of a culture of equality, in Tocqueville's view, is that it can become "leveling" if the people, motivated by envy, try to create equality by tearing everything down to their level.

According to Tocqueville, the democratic resentment of anything that seems to place one individual above the common level extended to politics. American politicians, no matter how distinguished their accomplishments or how superior their leadership skills, had to pretend to be just a common man in order to get elected. Any hint that they considered themselves *worthy* of high office because of their merits would cause equality-obsessed American voters to reject them. This had at least one very bad consequence, according to Tocqueville: American democracy tended to put mediocre people in public office. Idealistic advocates of democracy, such as Thomas Jefferson, had always argued that democracy would find and elevate the best people into positions of power. Tocqueville was sorry to report that this is not the case. Instead, he "discovered with astonishment that good qualities were common among the governed but rare among the rulers" in the America of his day. There were distinguished and talented individuals in America, but they tended not to get elected and usually didn't even run for office. One reason for this was the American resentment of anything or anyone that seemed "elitist." Many talented individuals simply decided that the process of bowing and scraping before a suspicious public, just to get elected, was an indignity they could live without.

Universities seem, by their very nature, to be elitist institutions, so they will always be in a precarious position in a democracy. They will have some trouble justifying themselves before democratic publics or legislatures. While aristocracies cherished sublime notions of human perfection, according to Tocqueville, and were very open to the notion of knowledge for its own sake—"liberal education" was invented for the European aristocracy—democracies tend to cherish only things that are profitable or useful. In a democracy, the tastes and preferences of the majority prevail, and the majority is primarily interested in wealth and comfort. If democratic legislatures fund universities, it will likely be because they are seen as engines of economic growth and technological progress, not because they are centers for the development of the higher faculties of the mind. If the children of a democracy attend universities, it will likely be because they are told that is the way to get a higher paying job. Some of those students may discover better reasons while at university, but that will not change the wider democratic culture.

Democratic culture, Tocqueville says, will have a similar effect on literature and the arts. The arts, which were at the center of aristocratic culture, will likely languish in democracy because they are not considered "useful." Great literature will be almost supplanted by easily digested, emotionalistic "bestsellers" that appeal to the majority. Overall, following the priorities of the majority, a democratic culture will be materialistic and oriented toward economic progress above all else. Phenomena like this are what led Tocqueville to say that the majority rules utterly and without opposition in America—"like God over the universe." They control not only politics but also virtually every aspect of life. There are very positive aspects to democratic culture, and Americans have succeeded in counteracting some of the bad things that also result from it. They have alleviated its materialism with their religious traditions, and they have combated the selfish "individualism" it can foster by cultivating citizenship. But clearly, in order to understand American democracy well, we have to come to grips with all the features of its distinctive political culture.

Essay #2
Liberalism and the U. S. Constitution

The problem with democracy is the same as with any form of government: the people in power are liable to abuse that power. When the majority is in power, the rights of the minority--anyone who is not in the majority on a given issue--can be threatened. As you already know from Chapter I, the great problem in democracy is the threat of what later came to be called the tyranny of the majority. The founders were acutely aware of this problem. They faced the task of constructing a popular government that would somehow prevent the majority from abusing its power. How could this be done when there is no monarch or aristocracy to check and balance popular power? As James Madison said in his famous essay, Federalist #10, if this problem could not be solved, democracy would have to be abandoned as a form of government. For once again, in the philosophy of liberalism, the protection of individual rights is more important than any form of government, including democracy.

Madison's Federalist #10 is the classic statement of the way the Constitution seeks to solve the problem of democracy. Madison there identifies the problem as majority faction. In Madison's definition, a faction is any group that desires something contrary to the rights of individuals or the common good (a Madisonian faction is different from an interest group, which may or may not be harmful to rights or the common good). The problem arises when a faction becomes the majority in a democratic system: can it be prevented from implementing its evil designs? Pure democracy offers no solution to this problem. But Madison says the Constitution sets up not a democracy, but a republic, where the people rule indirectly through representatives. The Founders regarded representation to be one of the great innovations of modern political science, and it is important to recognize the role it plays in American democracy. Madison regards representation as a kind of filter. In his view, the role of representatives is not to translate the people's wishes directly into law, but to exercise some independent judgment. They should even prevent the people's wishes from becoming law if the people want something stupid or unjust. Madison and the other Framers of the Constitution hoped that the people would elect intelligent and public-spirited representatives whose judgment and virtue would be superior to that of the populace at large. Under the Constitution, representatives have the power to defy public opinion if a factious majority forms. Madison and the Framers hoped and expected that laws passed by representatives would actually be better than laws passed directly by the people.

The Framers did not rely exclusively on representation to solve the problem of majority faction. Madison argued that a large country like the United States would have a better chance of escaping majority faction just because its diversity would prevent any one group from becoming a majority and capturing the government. And the reason the Framers created a system of checks and balances within the government was to prevent elected officials from abusing their power if they proved not to be the kind of superior representative Madison hoped for. Still, Madison's view is that representatives should be a kind of elite, and that representation is partly a democratic, partly an anti-democratic, institution. From this point of view, the Constitution is an ingenious mechanism for consulting public opinion regularly, without allowing it to control anything directly. The Constitution is based on the idea that government should be rooted in popular will, but that public opinion and public judgment are too unreliable to serve as a direct source of government policy. Some state constitutions provide for initiative or referendum, in which citizens get to vote directly on issues of public policy. Under the Federal Constitution, by contrast, citizens are never asked directly what they think about policy issues. They are only asked whom they trust to make decisions for them--whom they want to represent them. This is not an oversight. It is a deliberate decision, based on the Framers' assessment of the shortcomings of democracy, and the best ways to deal with them.

During the debate over the adoption of the Constitution, the opponents of the document did not fail to notice its approach to democracy. There was lively public debate over the Constitution, with the so-called anti-federalists opposing it. Some of the anti-federalists charged the Constitution with being a betrayal of democracy and the principles of the Revolution of 1776. They admitted that democracy had problems, but argued that the solution was to make the system more democratic. They thought that the key to successful democracy was making (or keeping) the people virtuous, so they would not abuse their power. Then the government should be tied to the people as closely as possible, on the supposition that more direct input by the people would keep the government more in line. The anti-federalists wanted to keep greater power in the states and localities, where people could keep more of an eye on government. They feared that the proposed federal government would be too remote, would escape from popular control, and possibly degenerate into a tyranny. The anti-federalists lost the debate on ratification of the Constitution, but they did force the addition of a bill of rights to the document, further guaranteeing against the abuse of power by the federal government.

States have sometimes experimented with more direct democracy. The Texas Constitution represents a kind of experiment in "anti-federalist" government. The members of the Texas constitutional convention of 1875-76 (the current constitution was approved by voters in 1876) were not as philosophically sophisticated as the earlier anti-federalists, but they were very suspicious of government power, and believed that the best way to control government was to tie it closely to the people. The document they drafted reflects these concerns. While initiative and referendum are not provided for in the Texas constitution, there are many other ways in which the people have tighter control over state government than they do over the federal government. The Texas constitution is very detailed, so that policy decisions often require constitutional amendments--and such amendments must be voted on directly by the people. Many of the executive officers of the state, such as the Lieutenant Governor, attorney general and the commissioner of agriculture are independently elected by voters. Similar offices at the federal level are filled by presidential appointment and senate confirmation. Most judges in Texas are elected, also in contrast to the federal system of appointment and confirmation. And the state legislature meets in regular session only once every two years, for a limited period. On the whole, the Texas system is designed to discourage anyone from making a career of state politics. The idea is that government should be run by ordinary people who return to their work after serving the state or between sessions of the state legislature, rather than by a class of professional politicians. Compared to the federal constitution, the Texas constitution is more democratic: it puts more faith in popular opinion, and less faith in the ability of government to limit itself.

PRO & CON
Is American Democracy Sick?

Tocqueville wrote his book to show how the Americans of his day had overcome most of the problems inherent in democracy. In doing so, he gave us a yardstick to measure the health of American democracy today. This has sparked a lively debate over whether American democracy at the dawn of the 21st Century remains healthy or is not in good shape. *Who is correct?*

American Democracy is Not in Good Shape.
Alexis de Tocqueville praised the Americans of his day for developing a culture that could support a healthy democracy. The Americans of our day have weakened or abandoned so many of those old cultural attributes that we have real reason to be alarmed about the future of our democracy. Some particulars:

Citizenship. Our ancestors, according to Tocqueville, learned the skills of responsible self-government in the school of local, township governance. But how many Americans today even know what is going on in their local government? Maybe it's because Americans move around so much that they don't have local roots anymore. Maybe it's because the federal government has taken control of so many things that used to be the responsibility of local government. Tocqueville did warn that central government could easily destroy the vibrancy of local government by taking over too many of its powers. Isn't this exactly what has happened? Overall, Americans have become too apathetic, too "individualistic" in Tocqueville's sense. They are too wrapped up in their own personal concerns and too interested in their own private enjoyments to shoulder the burdens of citizenship. Unfortunately, we have become more like the European peasants Tocqueville describes, passively waiting for government to solve our problems or give us handouts without taking any personal responsibility for making the system work. Finally, Tocqueville praises the Americans of the 1830s for their ability to form political associations, yet studies today suggest that American individualism has gotten to the point that we are losing this ability too. Fewer and fewer people take an active role in any kind of association, political or otherwise. This does not bode well for the future of American democracy.

Religion and Morality. Tocqueville argued that a solid moral code is needed in democracy and that religion is a necessary support for it. It has almost become a cliché today to say that the nation is suffering from "moral decay," which is precisely a weakening of the moral backbone we used to have. Religion was so strong in Tocqueville's day that he claimed no one would dare say they were an atheist. Today, by contrast, in large segments of American culture, people would be ashamed to admit they are religious. On Tocqueville's analysis, this is a very worrisome development. It was his view that, in society at large, religion is the only solid and long-lasting basis for morality. If religion declines, public morality will eventually follow. One thing he found remarkable in the United States of his day was the lack of sexually explicit material, or pornography. It was not outlawed, but Americans' moral code simply did not allow it to exist. Clearly, things have changed in this country. The rise in crime rates, drug use, teenage pregnancy, and the like, show that the strong moral code that once restrained individuals in this country is unraveling. As Tocqueville said, healthy democracy depends on people policing themselves, but Americans seem less and less capable of doing that.

American Democracy is in Fine Shape.

Citizenship. Things have certainly changed, and it is more difficult to get involved in local government now. Most Americans live in cities that can't be governed like the old New England townships. But when important issues come before even the largest city government, citizens show up to let their voices be heard. Americans have not lost their great ability to form associations for political purposes. Some studies suggest that Americans are more politically engaged than the citizens of other democracies. Not only do we have massive national groups like the Sierra Club and the National Rifle Association, but also local associations that form all the time. These local associations promote environmental causes, influence zoning ordinances, and address myriad other problems. I'm sure all of us have had the experience of being presented with a petition supporting some political cause at a shopping mall or other public place. In states like California, where propositions can be placed on the statewide ballot by signature-gathering initiatives, there seems to be no shortage of grass-roots activism. American voting may be declining, but that is only one aspect of citizenship. On Tocqueville's scale of active citizenship, we are not doing badly.

Religion and Morality. America remains the most religious of all the developed Western democracies, as Americans remain almost Puritanical in their social morality, compared to European nations. If you've ever visited a European country and seen the prurient images in advertising or on television, you know this is true. Further, the United States actually seems to have gotten *more* religious and moral over the last generation or two. It was true that many college students a generation ago would feel ashamed to say they're religious, but now religious groups on campus are very visible. Social attitudes toward things like teenage pregnancy and drug use are actually becoming stricter, and some evidence indicates that those problematic behaviors are decreasing. In politics, candidates for office are almost expected to profess religious beliefs, which was not true even ten years ago. Tocqueville would be proud—we are practically in the midst of a Puritan revival! But why are we so obsessed with religion anyway? Who says you have to be religious to be moral? For Tocqueville, after all, social morality is the important thing, not religion *per se*. For many people, their religion is inseparable from their morality, but for others, it is not. Our increased toleration of morally sound individuals of every stripe is actually an improvement over 1830.

EXERCISE 2-1

Read the Pro and Con essays on the previous page, and think about which side makes more sense to you. Think of three experiences you have had or things you have observed (this could include the attitudes of people around you on citizenship or morality) that support your view of this matter. Briefly describe those experiences or observations below, and explain how they support your position.

1. _____

_____

_____

_____

_____

2. _____

_____

_____

_____

_____

3. _____

_____

_____

_____

_____

Name	Seat	Score

EXERCISE 2-2
Religion and Society on the Web

Two groups that are contending over the proper role of religion in society are the Christian Coalition and Americans United for Separation of Church and State.

Go to the websites of the Christian Coalition (http://cc.org/) and Americans United for Separation of Church and State (http://www.au.org/).

Pick some current issue that both address, and briefly describe the positions they take. What do you think Tocqueville would have to say about the issue?

_____

_____

_____

_____

_____

_____

_____

_____

_____

_____

_____

_____

_____

_____

_____

_____

_____

Name		Seat	Score

EXERCISE 2-4
Political Culture and Democracy in Iraq

Imagine you are an advisor to the post-Saddam Hussein government of Iraq. Using insights from Alexis de Tocqueville, compose a short list of challenges you think the Iraqi people may confront on their way to democracy. Can you suggest solutions to any of these problems?

_____

_____

_____

_____

_____

_____

_____

_____

_____

_____

_____

_____

_____

_____

_____

_____

Name	Seat	Score

EXERCISE 2-5
Representatives as Filters

In the second essay in this chapter, the author writes "Madison regards representation as a kind of filter. In his view, the role of representatives is not to translate the people's wishes directly into law, but to exercise some independent judgment. They should even prevent the people's wishes from becoming law if the people want something stupid or unjust."

To encourage you to think about representatives as filters rather than as delegates (who do what a majority of the public prefers), think of an issue, either historical or current, and discuss the actions of Congress in Madison's terms. Explain how Congress served as a filter of public sentiment, or failed to serve as a filter of opinion, on the issue you selected.

Of course there are many other issues, but here are some controversial issues about which you may write if you are having trouble coming up with an example of your own:

- A Constitutional amendment to forbid desecration of the American flag
- The War in Vietnam
- Stem cell research
- Federal gun control
- The War with Iraq
- Laws forbidding teaching of Native American languages
- Laws prohibiting federal payments for abortion services

_____

_____

_____

_____

_____

_____

_____

_____

_____

_____

_____

_____

Name		Seat	Score

THE U. S. CONSTITUTION:
NOT JUST FOR THE UNITED STATES ANYMORE?
James Meernik

The U.S. Constitution has proved to be one of the most durable and malleable founding documents in the history of the world. We have reinterpreted and modified the Constitution in many ways to meet the demands of the growing and changing American society. For example, in 1954 the Supreme Court determined in the landmark *Brown v. Board of Education* decision that segregation of the races was at odds with the cherished principles of equality found in the Constitution. Justices of the Supreme Court have interpreted the Constitution as guaranteeing a woman's right to have an abortion as well as our right to burn the American flag, even though there is no explicit mention of such things in the Constitution. I could provide many other examples of how our interpretation of the Constitution has changed over time. Equally important, however, has been the expansion of the reach of the United States Constitution. That is, to whom does the Constitution apply? We have become accustomed to thinking that the Constitution applies to all citizens of the United States, and certainly that is true. Yet, in the past, rights provided us by the Constitution did not extend to all Americans. Slaves and Native Americans did not enjoy all the privileges and protections offered by the Constitution. And it was not until the 1920s that the Supreme Court began to rule that the states and cities of this country were bound to respect the people's civil liberties as enshrined in the Bill of Rights. Thus, one story of the U. S. Constitution is its ever-broadening reach to affect the lives of more and more people. That trend continues today in ways of which many American citizens may not even be aware.

The story I would like to relate to you is an account of the exporting of the U.S. Constitution to reach the citizens and governments of foreign countries. It may surprise you to learn that many of our laws and the international laws our government has accepted allow for the peoples of other nations to use U.S. courts to hear their grievances. It may seem troubling, or at least unusual to many of you, to learn that our courts have opened their doors in this manner. In fact, this expansion of the reach of the U.S.

Constitution has evolved in a fairly predictable and reasonable way, given the history of our nation. The goal of this chapter is to explain how and why we—you and I and our government— have worked to "secure the blessings of liberty" for people in other lands. So rather than provide you with a dry dissection of the text of the U.S. Constitution, I believe your understanding and appreciation of the Constitution would be better improved by exploring the values embedded in it. Are these values—our political ideals—universal in nature and to be enjoyed by people the world over? Or, are they American values based on our culture and history, which should therefore remain within our shores? Ponder these questions as we proceed.

Constitutional Protections for Americans Overseas

Let us first review what should be some of the more obvious instances in which the U.S. Constitution applies to events in foreign countries. First, our American embassies and consulates overseas are given the legal status of American territory so that U.S. laws govern whatever happens inside these places. The fact that U.S. laws apply within the walls of our embassies and consulates also means that, generally, those foreign citizens who flee into them requesting asylum from their governments can seek the protection of American laws. Diplomats and other U.S. government personnel who work in these embassies, as well as other U.S. public employees working and traveling overseas on official business, are generally given "diplomatic immunity." This means that when they violate the laws of their host nation, foreign governments will routinely waive their right to prosecute these Americans under their own laws. Of course, our government provides the same protections to the representatives of foreign governments working in this country. Sometimes, though, in very controversial cases where a representative of a foreign government breaks the law of the host country, that host government may ask to try the diplomat in its courts. You may recall an incident a few years ago involving a representative of the

Ukrainian government who was charged with drunk driving in New York. The government of Ukraine waived that man's diplomatic immunity and allowed his case to be tried in an American court.

Members of the U.S. armed forces who are stationed overseas and who violate the laws of their host nations are almost always tried in a U.S. military court martial hearing. But what about their relatives who accompany them to the U.S. military base overseas? Who prosecutes them when they violate the law? In a famous Supreme Court case from 1957, *Reid v. Covert* (354 S.1), the justices ruled that the wife of a member of the U.S. armed forces stationed overseas was entitled to a trial in a U.S. civilian court for an alleged murder. The U.S. military had wanted to try her in a U.S. military court martial proceeding in Germany, where her husband was stationed. The U.S. Supreme Court held that the U.S. law, which had given this power to the Department of Defense, was unconstitutional because Congress could not deny to ordinary American citizens their constitutional rights to a trial by jury and other procedural rights that were not available under a court martial proceeding. Justice Black wrote that the United States *"can only act in accordance with all the limitations imposed by the Constitution"* (354 U.S. at 6). Therefore, when the United States government possesses authority over its citizens abroad, it must provide them with all the same rights and privileges U.S. citizens enjoy at home (Henkin, 1996, 547 note 84).

Of course, nearly all the time when private American citizens traveling in other countries break laws, they are tried in the courts of those nations. You may recall the incident a few years ago when an American teenager was given a "caning" in Singapore for acts of vandalism. A caning is a beating on the back with a stick. This young man was not protected against any type of "cruel and unusual punishment," which is prohibited in this country by the Eighth Amendment, because the U.S. Constitution does not take precedence over the ordinary laws of other countries. Interestingly, many Americans supported the decision by the Singapore court because they felt it was a deserved punishment. Similarly, if you, as a U.S. citizen, are the victim of a crime in another country, you must rely upon the court system in that nation for any kind of justice or restitution in most instances. Any

exceptions to what is known in legal terms as "foreign sovereign immunity"—the right of any government to apply its own laws in its own country without oversight by another government—must be provided for in a U.S. treaty with that nation. In fact, most of these exceptions concern issues relating to commerce and trade. Lastly, it is worth mentioning for those of you who like to travel to the remote regions of the earth, that United States laws also do not apply to lands that are not part of any country. The U.S. Supreme Court ruling in 1933 in *Smith v. United States* (507 U.S. 197) involved a lawsuit filed by a woman whose husband fell in a crevice while hiking in Antarctica. To collect damages for her husband's death, the widow alleged that the U.S. government was responsible for his accident because: 1) Antarctica was not a foreign land and therefore subject to certain U.S. laws and 2) the U.S. government should have posted more signs in Antarctica warning of the hazards of hiking. She lost when the Supreme Court ruled that the U.S. government was not responsible for accidents that happened abroad, even if the lands were not a foreign "nation" as such.

Constitutional Protections
For Foreign Citizens

The use of American laws and certain constitutional protections in disputes involving foreign citizens is, for the most part, a recent phenomenon in American history. Yet the seeds of this fascinating development were planted when the ink on the U.S. Constitution was barely dry. In 1789 the first U.S. Congress passed the Alien Tort Claims Act (ATCA), which reads in part, "The district courts shall have original jurisdiction of any civil action by an alien for a tort only, committed in violation of the law of nations or a treaty of the United States" (cited in Mattei and Lena, 2001:384). The Alien Tort Claims Act essentially allows aliens—that is, citizens of foreign countries—to bring "torts", or a civil action seeking compensation and punitive damages because of a violation or wrongdoing by another party. The key is that aliens are only allowed to bring such suits for violations of the "law of nations" or a treaty to which the United States is a party. Certainly there are many subjects in international law that an alien might wish to bring into an American court, but the U.S. courts have been fairly strict in determining which violations of the law of nations and international treaties can be brought into our courts. Scholars believe that the Congress originally passed the law to allow the United States to hear cases involving international piracy (Mattei and Lena, 2001:384) that affected all nations using the oceans for commerce.

Before a U.S. court can take jurisdiction, however, several requirements must be met. First, the case must involve a subject of the "law of nations" or a treaty to which the United States is a party. Only when the alleged violation relates to "well established, universally recognized norms of international laws" can a U.S. court hear the case (see *Filartiga* v. *Pena-Irala,* 630 F.2d 881). According to The Restatement (Third) of the Foreign Relations Law of the United States, there are several crimes that our government considers to be part of the law of nations, including: "genocide; slavery or slave trade; murder or causing the disappearance of individuals; torture or other cruel, inhuman, or degrading treatment or punishment; prolonged arbitrary detention; systematic racial discrimination; or a consistent pattern of gross violations of internationally recognized human rights" (cited in Morrin, 2000:432). Second, the accused must be present in the United States. Third, the judges must determine that an American court is an appropriate place to settle the dispute. If the courts in the victim's home country are fair and impartial, the U.S. court will likely not hear the tort claim. On the other hand, if the courts in the victim's home country are biased or dominated by a government that does not provide protections for the accused and may even seek to harm the victim, the U.S court may decide it will hear the case.

Perhaps the most important area of international law where judges have determined that aliens are allowed to bring torts involves international prohibitions against torture. In 1980, in the case of *Filartiga* v. *Pena-Irala*, two citizens of the Latin American country of Paraguay brought a tort against a Paraguayan government official, alleging that he had tortured and killed a relative. Because the defendant, Mr. Pena-Irala, was in the United States on a visitor's visa, it was possible to bring the tort against him. The U.S. district court that heard the case found that:

Deliberate torture perpetrated under color of official authority, violates universally accepted norms of the international law of human rights, regardless of the nationality of the parties. Thus, whenever an alleged torturer is found and served with process by an alien within our borders, section 1350 provides federal jurisdiction (Ibid at 878).

The District Court argued that, because torture is universally condemned in several international conventions and other agreements, it is a recognized principle of the law of nations, and therefore, it is an appropriate subject for the ATCA. Also, because it is likely that the very government that tortured the individual would be unlikely to allow that person a fair hearing, there is a good chance the U.S. would accept jurisdiction because the torture victim might fear for her life should she return home. In another important case, Bosnian Muslim women who had been raped during the war in Bosnia in the 1990s brought a lawsuit against Radovan Karadzic, the Bosnian Serb leader whom they charged was ultimately responsible for these crimes (see *Kadic* v. *Karadzic,* 70F.3d 232). Their case was heard because rape is considered a form of torture; the accused was present in New York City for a meeting at the United Nations, and it was unlikely the women could obtain a fair hearing, or a hearing at all, in their home country, which was at war. The women were ultimately awarded $745 million in damages (Westlaw).

Individuals who are citizens of other countries and who suffer from violations of international law committed by an American business or individual can also have their claims heard in American courts. In another case applying the Alien Tort Claims Act, *National Coalition Government of the Union of Burma v. Unocal, Inc.,* a U.S. District court ruled that citizens of Burma could take an American corporation, Unocal, to court for violations of their rights (176 F.R.D.329, 349). The Burmese citizens who filed the suit called themselves the National Coalition Government of the Union of Burma to distinguish themselves from what they believed was the illegitimate government of Burma, or Myanmar, as it is now known. These individuals argued that Unocal and the government of Myanmar engaged in torture and forced labor while Unocal was building a natural gas pipeline in Myanmar. While these individuals did not ultimately win any damages, the U.S. court did rule that it had a right to hear their grievance against the American corporation. Many believe that, through the use of the ATCA, American-owned multinational corporations can be forced to adhere to international human rights standards when they operate in foreign countries. Otherwise, it is feared these businesses will engage in questionable and illegal labor practices that they would be prevented from using in the United States.

Another way in which foreign citizens can have their claims heard in U.S. courts is through The Torture Victim Protection Act (TVPA), which became U.S. law in 1991. Under the TVPA, foreign citizens and American citizens are allowed to bring suits "against any individual who, under actual or apparent authority or under color of law of any foreign nations, subjects any individual to torture or extrajudicial killing" (in Stephens, 2001:942-943). Extrajudicial killings are state-sanctioned or state-supported murders outside of the normal procedures of a criminal justice system (such as a court sentence of execution). An important part of this Act is that only individuals, not governments, can be charged with torture or extrajudicial killings. In addition, former heads of state can be prosecuted for violating the TVPA, but current heads of state are immune from prosecution. It is also possible to use the Torture Victim Protection Act for alleged violations that took place prior to its passage in 1991. Normally, this kind of retroactive prosecution would be considered unconstitutional since it violates the protection against ex post facto laws (laws that make something a crime only after the act has been committed). But a U.S. district court ruled that since torture had long been considered an international crime, the defendants should have known that what they were doing was wrong, even if the TVPA was not an American law yet. This Act complements the Alien Tort Claims Act not only by supporting lawsuits against torture but also by adding protection against extrajudicial killings.

No doubt many of you are scratching your heads and wondering if the American judicial system is capable of handling all the different torts that alien citizens might bring to them. Undoubtedly, there are hundreds, if not thousands, of incidents that might qualify under the ATCA. *Can* the overworked U.S. courts handle all these cases? *Should* they be handling these cases? The second question will be discussed in the Pro/Con Essay at the conclusion of this chapter, so I will address the first question here. First, we must keep in mind that only when the person or organization charged with violating the law of nations is physically in the United States will U.S courts take jurisdiction. The foreign citizen who brings the tort must be present as well. Naturally, any foreign citizen who believes he or she might be sued in a U.S. court under the ATCA would probably avoid travel to the United States. Second, the U.S. courts have recognized that they will need to be careful to prevent an overload of cases from clogging the system and transporting international disputes into the U.S. judicial system. The American courts have been very selective about which cases they will hear. Indeed, in the case involving Radovan Karadzic described earlier, the Second Circuit Court of Appeals ruled that judges should, *"…act where appropriate in light of the express legislative mandate of the Congress…without compromising the primacy of the political branches in foreign affairs"* (see *Kadic v. Karadzic*, 70 F.3d at 248-249). That is, the courts should avoid becoming involved in disputes that might interfere with the conduct of American foreign policy.

What Explains the Extension of the Constitution?

The Framers of the U.S. Constitution were not only great scholars of the political philosophies of their day, but they were also quite well versed in international law. While international agreements were much fewer and more limited in the late 18th Century, the Founding Fathers believed that the United States had a duty to abide by them. Hence, they wrote in the Supremacy clause in Article VI of the Constitution that international treaties were to be considered the law of the land. Furthermore, in Article I they gave Congress the power to define offences against the law of nations. And of course, it was the Founding Fathers who authored the Alien Tort Claims Act. Many, if not most of them, believed that their experiment in democracy was an example for other nations to imitate. It should come as no surprise that they were prepared to extend some of the blessings of liberty to their foreign brethren.

The Founding Fathers were generally content for the United States to stand as a "shining city on the hill" to attract freedom-loving people and to serve as an enlightened example for other peoples around the world. Later generations of American leaders have been much more willing to actively assist other peoples in the quest for justice and freedom. The United States embarked on many military interventions in the western hemisphere in the early 20th Century to help democratize the nations of Central America and the Caribbean. Since the 1980s the U.S. government has spent billions of dollars promoting democracy throughout the world through foreign aid, military intervention, and other programs encouraging respect for the rule of law. The use of the Alien Tort Claims Act and the Torture Victim Protection Act is, in many ways, just one more tool our government has to convince other nations that democracy in general, and a fair and impartial judiciary in particular, are good for everyone. In fact, this American need to convince others of the exceptional value of our institutions and ideals is not unique in the history of the world. As Hans Morgenthau (1973:10) wrote, *"All nations are tempted and few have been able to resist the temptation for long—to clothe their own particular aspirations and actions in the moral purposes of the universe."* Using the U.S. judicial system to settle disputes among citizens of foreign countries is part of a long tradition of exporting our most cherished values.

This use of international law and courts to resolve disputes among people and nations is only going to increase in the future. Just recently, the International Criminal Tribunal came into existence with the power to hear cases involving war crimes, crimes against humanity, and genocide that occur anywhere in the world. The United States is not a party to the treaty because it fears what might happen if the Court were allowed to prosecute American soldiers and civilians stationed overseas. It is somewhat ironic that the United States, which has sought to use its courts to settle disputes among foreign citizens, is unwilling to allow an international tribunal any right to hear cases involving its citizens. A majority of the nations of the world, however, believe that only through the creation of an international criminal tribunal can we hold individuals accountable for atrocities such as we witnessed in the former Yugoslavia, Sierra Leone, and East Timor. In addition, some nations, especially in Europe, have passed laws providing for what is known as "universal jurisdiction." The courts of these nations, such as Belgium and Switzerland, are now allowed to hear cases involving any violation of international law, no matter where it has occurred and who it involved. For example, in cases of genocide that occurred in Rwanda between Rwandan citizens, Belgian courts have tried the perpetrators. Clearly, the trend in the world is to create and use the best possible judicial systems to resolve conflicts. As the United States has taken the lead in peaceful conflict resolution through the courts since its founding, it is probably only a matter of time before it once again becomes a strong advocate of the international rule of law. The forces behind what has come to be known as "judicial globalization" are many and powerful.

PRO & CON
Should U.S. Courts Hear Cases Involving Foreign Citizens?

YES. U.S. courts should hear disputes involving foreign citizens first and foremost because our laws allow it, and we must obey the law. Both our Founding Fathers, who passed the Alien Tort Claims Act, and our modern day legislators and judges have understood that it is in the interest of all American citizens that the nation obey those international laws that our leaders have signed. And it is only when foreign citizens are involved in controversies related to these international laws that our courts can become involved. Thus, our own laws and our international agreements bind us. The Framers of the Constitution must have understood the value of living up to these agreements or they would not have given international treaties the same status in the Constitution as our national legislation.

Allowing foreign citizens access to our courts also can help promote human rights all over the world. We can all agree that crimes such as torture and state-sponsored murder should be condemned everywhere they occur. But the reality is that many countries in the world routinely engage in such behavior. The courts in these countries are either tools of the government used to help commit atrocities or they are too afraid to protect the rights of individuals against despotic governments. By holding officials in these governments accountable for their international crimes and educating the world about their heinous acts through public trials, we may one day cause these governments to stop abusing their own people. We should not sit by and watch while these crimes are committed, but we should use our courts to help put an end to them. Evil triumphs when good people do not take action.

Finally, many governments in the world are beginning to recognize that one of the most effective tools we have to combat torture, genocide, war crimes, and the like is our courts. Rather than always settling our disputes and dealing with noxious governments by going to war, we might better address some of the world's problems through fair and open trials. That is why there is now an International Criminal Court that will soon be hearing cases involving genocide, crimes against humanity, and war crimes. That is why more governments are passing laws that allow their courts to hear any cases involving a violation of certain international laws. The United States was a leader in this trend as far back as 1789 and as recently as the mid-1990s when it helped establish the international criminal tribunals for the former Yugoslavia and Rwanda. It is time we helped lead the way again so that we have a voice in how disputes are to be resolved in world courts rather than remaining passive on the sidelines while the world moves on without us.

NO. In a perfect world where American courts had little to do, where our judges and juries understood all the causes and consequences of complex events in foreign countries, and where all the world accepted our vision of justice, it might be worthwhile allowing U.S. courts to hear cases involving foreign citizens. But it is not a perfect world. First, our courts are already busy dealing with thousands of cases each year. We already have our hands full with the war on drugs, white-collar crime, and terrorism, not to mention all the lawsuits Americans file. Do we really have the time, energy, and resources to take on the rest of the world's problems? And even if the number of cases involving foreign citizens that are heard today is small, who knows how many there will be in the future?

Second, it seems incredible that we would want our judges and juries to begin making decisions about the responsibility of individuals for complicated events that occur thousands of miles from our shores. We know most Americans are only dimly aware of the world around them. Would we want these same individuals trying to sort out the political, criminal and legal problems faced by people we know almost nothing about? It is probably not possible or desirable for people or courts anywhere in the world to begin conducting trials involving foreigners. If we do not understand the problems we wish our courts to solve, we may just make things worse by trying to sort these problems out.

Finally, I think we can all agree that the United States should not be in the business of enforcing its own values and legal proceedings on people who have not freely consented. Americans would probably all be opposed to a foreign government hearing disputes involving our citizens. Why should we expect other people to agree to such things? It is this kind of "we know best" attitude that many in the world find offensive about the United States. Whether we like it or not, the rest of the world does not always share our values. In fact, if our values are universal, we should be able to promote them through education, not impose them through the courts.

EXERCISE 3-3
Subject Review

The following questions will test your knowledge of the United States Constitution. Select the best answer for each question.

1. _____ Which branch of government is given the power to declare war?
   A. The President
   B. The Supreme Court
   C. The Department of Defense
   D. The Congress

2. _____ Judgment by the Senate in cases of impeachment is limited to
   A. monetary damages
   B. imprisonment
   C. removal from office
   D. forfeiture of citizenship

3. _____ In cases involving ambassadors and representatives of foreign governments, which court has the right to hear a case first?
   A. The Special Foreign Diplomats Court
   B. The U.S. Supreme Court
   C. Military court martial
   D. Federal district courts

4. _____ The President has the power to do what with respect to Congress?
   A. Adjourn a session of Congress
   B. Call for new elections
   C. Request the removal of certain members of Congress
   D. Order the House and Senate to merge into one body for extraordinary emergencies

5. _____ The States may not engage in which of the following:
   A. enter into a treaty or alliance with a foreign power
   B. regulate criminal activity
   C. regulate morticians
   D. pass laws providing for income taxes

6. _____ Which branch of government has the power to determine standards for weights and measures?
   A. The Supreme Court
   B. The Executive Branch
   C. The States
   D. The Congress

7. _____ The issue of slavery is dealt with in all *except* which of the following parts of the Constitution:
   A. Article I
   B. Article IV
   C. Thirteenth Amendment
   D. Article III

8. _____ Which part of the Constitution prohibits religious tests as a qualification for public office?
   A.   First Amendment
   B.   Ninth Amendment
   C.   Article I
   D.   Article VI

9. _____ If a president dies during his second year in office and the vice-president assumes the presidency, what is the maximum number of years the former vice president can hold office as president?
   A.   ten years
   B.   eight years
   C.   six years
   D.   four years

10. _____ What is the correct order of succession to the presidency?
   A.   Vice President, Speaker of the House, Senate Majority Leader
   B.   Vice President, President Pro Tempore of the Senate, Speaker of the House
   C.   Vice President, Speaker of the House, President Pro Tempore of the Senate
   D.   Secretary of State, Secretary of the Treasury, Secretary of Defense

Name		Seat	Score

THE BIRTH OF AMERICAN FEDERALISM
John A. Booth

"….The maintenance of the authority of the states over matters purely local is as essential to the preservation of our institutions as is the conservation of the supremacy of the Federal power in all matters entrusted to the nation by the Federal Constitution."*(Hammer* v. *Dagenhart*, 247 U.S. 251 (1918).

The United States is a nation originally constructed of thirteen separate fledgling nations, a fact that has shaped American government ever since. American government eventually developed a system known as federalism, in which a national or central (federal) government and constituent or regional (state) governments share sovereignty, authority, and ruling power.

The former British colonies (states), which declared themselves independent, initially viewed themselves as separate national entities rather than as subsidiaries of a larger whole. By 1776, each American colony had functioned for decades as a distinct society with its own government and traditions. However, because all the ex-colonies shared the immediate threat of having Britain as a larger, more powerful opponent of their independence, they quickly decided to work together.

Their shared need to defeat the British led the thirteen states to form a loose *confederation,* a weak association of separate, sovereign states. This arrangement became formal under the Articles of Confederation, which served as the first U.S. constitution until 1789. Under the Articles only the states were sovereign, i.e., all ruling power came from the states themselves. This kept the national government weak so the nation could not impose its will upon any state. Citizenship was only within each state, not the United States as a whole. Only state law governed individuals.

Eventually, many found this first U.S. government much too weak and dependent on the states. After one failed effort to revise the Articles, twelve states called a constitutional convention in May 1787, to draft a new governing document. The resulting Constitution of the United States of America, completed in September, 1787, and ratified in 1788, dramatically altered the relative powers of the states and the central (federal) government. Under this new federal system, ultimate sovereignty (the right to rule) would belong to the people, who would be citizens not only of their states but also of the new nation. By ratifying the Constitution, the American states created a federal government that would be supreme (note the Supremacy Clause in Article VI), with federal laws and treaties to prevail over those of the states. The new federal government would have a strong executive, a much strengthened Congress, and considerable direct authority over citizens.

In this arrangement, much had to be spelled out as to which powers the new federal government and the states would have or would be denied. The Constitution reserved certain powers exclusively to the federal government (e.g., to regulate commerce between the states, coin money, declare and make war, and negotiate treaties—see especially Article I, Section 8). Article I, Section 8 also contains the *elastic clause,* which gives the federal Congress the power "to make all laws which shall be necessary and proper" for executing its specified powers. The Constitution expressly denied certain powers to the federal government (bills of attainder, ex post facto laws, taxes on exports from the states, granting titles of nobility—Article I, Section 9). Some powers were explicitly denied to the states (such as to regulate foreign commerce, keep troops in peacetime, enter into foreign treaties— Article I, Section 10). The federal government and the states would share some powers, including the all-important right to levy taxes.

The *antifederalists* and others worried about the wide ranging new authority proposed for the new national government. In order to win ratification of the new Constitution, its advocates, the *federalists,* had to promise to limit its potentially vast powers over both citizens and the states by adding a Bill of Rights (ratified quickly by 1791). Amendments One through Eight specified many limits on federal government power. Two other amendments addressed the relationship among the citizens, states, and nation. Amendment Nine stated that the people retained other rights not spelled out in the Constitution. Very importantly for federal-state relations, Amendment Ten reserved much authority for the states by stating that the powers not delegated specifically to the federal government were "reserved to the states respectively, or to the people."

Evolving Federal-State Relations

Despite its detail, the Constitution and Bill of Rights did not leave federal-state relations clearly specified. Federal-state relationships have thus often prompted conflicts between the national and state governments. Over the long haul, the federal government has won increasing power and authority, entering many policy areas once considered the preserve of the states. Federal government power over the states has been expanded by five main devices:

a. Amendment of the U. S. Constitution;
b. Legislation enacted by Congress;
c. Rulings by the Supreme Court;
d. Fiscal (budgetary) initiatives by the federal government; and even
e. Force of arms.

This long-term tendency toward the expansion of federal power received a boost from the Thirteenth, Fourteenth, and Fifteenth Amendments after the Civil War but was curtailed significantly by a series of rulings by the U.S. Supreme Court in the late nineteenth and early twentieth centuries. But then for several decades beginning in the 1940s, federal power over the states again grew markedly. During this period, Congress often invoked its Constitutional authority to regulate interstate and foreign commerce as well as the Fourteenth Amendment to justify laws enhancing federal authority. States sometimes resisted the expanding federal role, yet also often embraced it—especially when Congress offered federal funds to cooperating states. During the 1980s and 1990s, however, the pendulum began swinging back toward the states. An increasingly conservative U.S. Supreme Court began overturning some federal laws that limited state sovereignty, and Congress itself began giving states more policy leeway. But when the Republican party gained control of the White House and both houses of Congress in the early 2000s, their support for states' rights eroded as they saw the advantage of the federal platform to promote certain preferred policies.

Federal-State Relations From the Perspective of Texas

One way to understand U. S. federalism is to look at it from the viewpoint of our own state. Shifting federal authority has affected Texas and Texans in innumerable areas. We will examine five:

1. *Slavery, Secession, and Reconstruction.* Texas entered the Union in 1846 as a slave state during the rapidly escalating debate over states' rights to maintain slavery. Many Texans joined other southerners in arguing that individual states could nullify (reject) national laws they did not accept, invoking state powers under the Articles of Confederation. Advocates of strong states' rights eventually led Texas to attempt secession with the Confederate States. In part, they argued that independent states had formed the union, so states had an inherent right to leave it. Many Texans fought for the Confederacy in support of this view of states' rights.

The Civil War (1861-1865) violently and definitively resolved this dispute for the Union and its federal government, and against the southern states' claims of rights to maintain slavery and nullify national policy. Victorious federal troops brought Texas back into the Union with the rest of the defeated Confederacy. The Union victory established once and for all federal government supremacy over the states. After that, the main question remaining was how vigorously the federal government would press its policy preferences upon the states. For a time after the war, the federal government strongly pursued changes in the South. Three new amendments to the U. S. Constitution dramatically altered social and economic relations and public policies in Texas (and the other southern states):

a. The Thirteenth Amendment (1865) abolished slavery;
b. The Fourteenth Amendment (1868) extended citizenship and Bill of Rights protection to citizens of the states, although many decades went by before these guarantees were meaningful; and
c. The Fifteenth Amendment (1870) prohibited the states from denying anyone the right to vote "on account of race, color, or previous condition of servitude."

These new requirements in the U.S. Constitution were enforced in Texas during Reconstruction (1865-1873). A state government dominated by pro-Union Texas Republicans enforced the Fourteenth and Fifteenth Amendments. The Reconstruction government integrated schools and gave freed slaves full citizenship so that they could vote and hold public office.

2. *Building Segregation.* Although the Union won the Civil War and asserted federal power during Reconstruction, the federal government retreated from this stance by the mid 1870s. This permitted states' rights conservatism and official racial bigotry to rise like phoenixes from the Confederacy's ashes. Because pro-slavery Texans had supported the Confederacy and strong rights for the states, they resented what they regarded as federal tampering with their society and government. Although Reconstruction temporarily stripped these Texans (mostly Democrats) of their political rights, they regained control of state and local government by 1876. Aided by a conservative U. S. Supreme Court that for several decades supported states' rights and relaxed federal supervision, racist Texas Democratic governments passed and implemented Jim Crow (segregationist) legislation. From the 1870s through the mid-twentieth century, the Texas Legislature repeatedly ignored the Fourteenth and Fifteenth Amendments' supposed protections of equal rights and did so with the tolerance of the U.S. Supreme Court. Texas passed many laws requiring racial segregation in education, housing, public services, and many other areas of life. The Legislature and officials also systematically undermined the citizenship and voting rights of Blacks. Poll taxes were instituted to discourage poor minorities from voting. The dominant Democratic Party instituted a white primary election so that minorities could not vote in key elections. Texas officials tolerated racial terrorism by the Ku Klux Klan, which violently intimidated minority citizens from participating in political life. For segregationist white Texans, the 1880s to the 1950s was an era of triumphant racism.

3. *Desegregation and Civil Rights.* From the late-nineteenth century until the mid-twentieth century, racial segregation prevailed in Texas. State law and local practice racially segregated housing and public schools. Segregation prevailed in many public and private domains including transportation, restaurants, hotels, theaters,

restrooms, drinking fountains, and cemeteries. Courts had separate facilities for (or outright denied service to) Blacks and sometimes to Hispanics. The Texas Democratic Party's primary election (the most important election in a state with virtually no Republican Party) barred Blacks from voting. Law and practice also barred minorities from juries, while multi-member districting systems kept minorities out of the legislature and off school boards and city councils.

Reversing its decades-long retreat from enforcing the Fourteenth and Fifteenth Amendments to the U. S. Constitution, the federal government in the 1950s began to press Texas and other states to end their racially discriminatory laws and practices. Prompted in part by the civil rights movement, federal pressure on Texas to desegregate came from the federal courts, Congress, and the executive branch.

Key court rulings advancing desegregation in Texas included the U. S. Supreme Court's 1944 ruling in *Smith v. Allwright* that the whites-only Texas Democratic Party primary election was unconstitutional. In 1950 The Supreme Court decreed that separate educational facilities for black University of Texas law student Herman Sweatt were inherently unequal and therefore unconstitutional (*Sweatt v. Painter*).

Sweatt laid legal groundwork for the landmark 1954 Kansas case, *Brown v. Board of Education of Topeka*, in which the Supreme Court outlawed all educational segregation and eventually ordered its end in Kansas and all other states as well. A constitutional amendment in 1964 and a ruling of the Supreme Court in 1966 (*Harper v. Virginia State Board of Education*) abolished the poll tax.

The U.S. Congress also passed laws to promote desegregation including the following:

- *The Civil Rights Act of 1964* made it illegal to discriminate on the basis of race, color, or national origin in public services, accommodations, and in employment (women were also covered by this section).

- *The Voting Rights Act of 1965* barred racial discrimination in voting, permitted federal officials to register state voters, and allowed them to monitor actual elections.

- The The 1975 renewal of the *Voting Rights Act* required bilingual elections to accommodate Spanish-speaking voters in Texas, outlawed districting systems and voting procedures that curtailed minority

41

representation, and greatly expanded federal supervision of Texas elections.

With these and many other mandates from the courts and Congress, often grounded in rights guaranteed by the Fourteenth Amendment of the U. S. Constitution, the federal executive branch heavily pressured Texas governments, schools and businesses to end racial discrimination. Many resisted, but eventually almost all *de jure* (legal) segregation was eliminated. Texas thus greatly opened up its elections and voter registration system, and eventually desegregated public services and accommodations, education, and juries.

De facto racial segregation and inequality (based on informal socioeconomic factors rather than legal discrimination) also declined because of federal pressure, but many areas and problems of unequal treatment remain in Texas. Texas minorities gained full political rights but still do not exercise them as much as the state's whites. Nor do minorities enjoy political influence proportionate to their numbers. Texas minorities remain poorer than their white counterparts, and informal segregation remains a critical problem in housing, education, and services. Nevertheless, almost all progress in reducing both *de facto* and *de jure* segregation in Texas has come from federal government pressures.

4. *Fiscal Federalism.* During the 1930s, the effects of the Great Depression on the national economy led the federal government to begin *fiscal federalism,* sharing its revenue with the states. The original goal of this program was to help states assist the needy and help put jobless people to work. Later, in the 1960s, President Lyndon Johnson's Great Society programs greatly expanded federal aid to the states. Hundreds of kinds of federal revenue transfers provided the states with assistance to fund welfare and medical assistance to the poor, health services, mass transit and highways, law enforcement, and community development, to name but a few. Such programs multiplied and expanded again in the 1970s.

In the area of fiscal federalism, Texas' state government usually did not resist federal intrusion as it had desegregation. Texas enthusiastically accepted most such federal revenue transfers and soon came to depend heavily on federal funds for many programs and services. By 1970, almost 30

percent of the Texas state government's income came from federal revenue transfers. When federal funding declined in the early 1980s, the Texas Legislature faced a cruel dilemma—either raise taxes to fund these programs or cut services. During the 1980s Texas taxpayers saw a fairly steady growth in their state tax burden—in significant measure to replace declining federal revenues. In the 1990s, federal transfers to Texas rose, but the recession of 2002 and shifting federal budget priorities again threatened to cut federal aid.

Federal authority over Texas has also expanded in many other policy arenas: environmental protection, defendants' rights, water and sewer treatment, prison conditions, transportation, urban development, regulation of the production and interstate transmission of oil and gas, voting rights, the drinking age, migrant workers' rights, and, most recently, education. In the 1980s, there emerged what was for Texas governments a new and distressing tendency in federal-state relations—unfunded federal mandates. Washington continued to impose costly new regulations and standards on other governments but ceased providing financial assistance to help pay for them. While many of the objectives of these mandates are laudable, they have heavily strained Texas governments and led to new conflicts between the state and the federal government.

5. *Devolution of power to the states.* The trend in relative federal-state power began to shift back toward the states beginning in the 1980s. The states and many conservatives (Republicans and Democrats) had long criticized unfunded federal mandates and advocated devolution (decentralization and return of power to the states). The emergence of a new conservative majority on the U.S. Supreme Court generally favored some devolution of power. The Court has begun to reject Congress's broad invocation of the Constitution's interstate commerce clause to justify intrusions into the states' policy space. In a case from San Antonio, *U.S. v. Lopez* (1995), the Court invalidated a law that regulated carrying guns near schools because the law was based on the commerce clause. That clause is a long-honored tool for expanding federal power, but the Supreme Court ruled that the gun ban had nothing to do with interstate commerce. In 1997

(*Printz v. United States*), the Court overturned part of the Brady Act because the justices held that it unconstitutionally required the states to administer a federal regulatory program. In 2003 the George W. Bush administration intervened in a lawsuit against the University of Michigan in opposition to its practice of affirmative action in admissions. Congress, too, has joined in the devolution trend. Texas gained new federal funds and more freedom to manage welfare in 1996 when Congress enacted welfare reform.

Devolution of power to the states is complicated. Though favorable toward reducing many federal mandates and regulations, social conservatives also advocate using federal law and regulations to promote other aspects of their agenda. The George W. Bush administration and its Republican majority in Congress have begun to turn away from supporting devolution. Following the September 11, 2001, terrorist attacks, federal regulatory control and programs have been strengthened. In 2005, Republicans in Congress led by Senate Majority Leader Bill Frist and House Majority Leader Tom Delay intervened in the Terry Schiavo "right to die" case. Congress hurriedly passed a law giving federal courts new jurisdiction to review such cases, thus imposing federal authority over a family law matter long the exclusive responsibility of the state courts.

Federalism and the Presidential Election of 2000

The U.S. Constitution gives the states the power to administer federal elections for president and members of Congress. The states have enacted differing election laws and practices that are usually administered by decentralized, county-level offices. Thus even in federal elections for the president and Congress, voting practices, ballot forms, counting mechanisms and technology, and contest procedures vary between and within states. Congress has subsequently enacted many restrictions and guidelines for the states' management of both federal and state elections, such as the Voting Rights Acts, but within those limits, the federal courts tend to defer to state laws and institutions when evaluating the conduct of elections.

In the 2000 presidential election between Republican candidate George W. Bush and Democratic candidate Al Gore, several extraordinary events transfixed the nation and revealed key tensions in federal-state relations. With the popular and electoral votes both very close nationwide, the national outcome of the election eventually came to turn on the results of Florida's popular vote, which was complicated by irregularities in both voting and the tallies in several counties. Even though Al Gore had a majority of the national popular vote, George W. Bush was a few hundred votes ahead in Florida. Whoever won the Florida popular vote would capture Florida's electors and the national Electoral College majority and thus win the presidency. For five tension-filled weeks after the November 7, 2000, election, the nation waited as the campaigns struggled for advantage in the Florida state and national arenas.

Gore and the Democrats believed that the state courts offered the best chance for success and fought under Florida law to have thousands of problematic untabulated votes from several counties hand-counted. Gore ultimately prevailed in the Florida Supreme Court, which ordered a last minute statewide hand tabulation of questioned ballots. Bush and the Republicans pursued a delaying strategy designed to exhaust the time for recounting. They asked federal courts to prevent hand tabulation and recounting, arguing that Florida's decentralized ballot scrutiny, without a uniform statewide standard, treated votes unequally and was inherently flawed. Most expert observers expected the U.S. Supreme Court to refuse the case in deference to state prerogatives to administer elections. The U.S. Supreme Court stunned the experts by accepting the case, and then, in a dramatic and closely divided 5-4 decision, stopped the Florida recount and hand tabulation. This gave Florida's electoral votes and the presidency to George W. Bush.

This dispute highlights several ironies related to federalism. First, a U.S. Supreme Court noted for its increasing deference to the states boldly reversed field and overturned Florida's 2000 presidential election contest process. Second, although federal authority limits the states' nominal power to conduct federal elections, that authority may be invoked only haphazardly or in close contests. Third, despite numerous federal election guidelines to the states, there exist no national procedural standards for election administration, counting, and contests in presidential and congressional votes. Thus, given our decentralized election administration, every presidential election is likely affected by undetected inequities and irregularities. And fourth, any effort to reform federal elections and rectify the voting problems revealed in 2000 will be very complex, involving as it must the U.S. Constitution, the Congress, and all fifty states. Any proposal to replace the Electoral College with direct popular presidential election will threaten a fundamental federalism provision of the Constitution, one designed to protect the smaller states' influence in choosing the president.

PRO & CON
Should the National-State Relationship Be Redefined and Powers Returned to the States?
Gloria C. Cox

Introduction: Conflict between the federal and state governments presents interesting and important dilemmas for public officials. Most observers believe that power has shifted substantially toward the federal government in the twentieth century, for reasons discussed in the preceding essay. Some officials and scholars favor examining the federal-state relationship and trying to re-establish a balance between the two centers of power. Ronald Reagan called for such changes, as did congressional Republicans when they regained control of the House and Senate in 1995. Has the power shift toward the federal government been good for the nation? Should power be returned to the states?

YES. Power should be returned to the states to renew the balance that once existed between federal and state governments. Although it may not be part of what you learned in your high school civics course, the fact is that the federal government has found new and innovative ways to seize power from the states and force the states to carry out federal policies in areas once reserved for state policies and action. These seizures of power are not constitutionally authorized, but Congress has found clever ways to mandate them anyway. Let's explore several examples in order to increase your understanding and knowledge about what is at stake in this debate.

- In 1984, Congress decided that young people should not be able to consume alcohol until they reach twenty-one years of age. The interest group Mothers Against Drunk Driving was instrumental in the fight; MADD waged an effective campaign to convince Congress that accidents, injuries, and fatalities from alcohol-related accidents would decrease if the drinking age were raised from eighteen to twenty-one.

    There was just one obstacle to the plan: Congress had no power to tell the states what the drinking age should be. No problem! Congress found a way around the lack of power in this issue area. It simply amended *The Transportation Act of 1982* to say that states would lose a portion of their federal highway funds if they failed to raise their drinking age. Voila! The drinking age was raised in one state after another (O'Connor and Sabato, 1997:99).

- In 1990 *The Americans With Disabilities Act* became law, requiring modification of businesses, schools, office buildings, museums, concert halls, and many other facilities to provide access to disabled persons. However, Congress failed to provide any funds to states or local governments to cover the costs associated with making those changes, many of which were expensive. This is a good example of the unfunded mandate discussed in the chapter essay. While the goals behind these laws are certainly commendable, the federal government abused the federal-state relationship by forcing states, counties, and cities to spend large sums of money to implement a policy that they had no hand in making. If Congress wanted to improve accessibility, it should have put money behind its policy.

- If you have renewed your driver's license or applied for some government benefit recently, you were probably asked if you wanted to register to vote. Ever wonder why state and county officials were making it so easy for you to register? It is readily explained by the fact that, in 1993, Congress passed and President Clinton signed *The National Voter Registration Act*, dubbed the Motor Voter bill. Even though voter registration is a state responsibility, the federal government stepped in to require that county and state personnel actively work to register voters. Once again, the federal government forced on the citizenry a law that Congress probably lacked the power to enact, and then required states to implement it.

Whether you believe that these policies are good ones for the nation--and most of you will probably agree that they are--they represent federal encroachments on state power. While these may seem like minor issues, the preponderance of power long ago shifted away from the states toward the national government. With each new transfer, the power differential widens further.

With such unfunded mandates as those relating to the Americans With Disabilities Act and voter registration, it is common for the federal government to accomplish its purposes by enacting requirements that the states (and local governments) must meet with their own funds. When such unfunded mandates are issued, states and localities have no choice but to reallocate funds from other purposes toward whatever Congress decides should take first priority. Fortunately for the states and local governments, unfunded mandates have gone out of fashion in recent years, having been opposed by Presidents Clinton and Bush.

It is important to remember that some of these policies may be welcome and useful, but the real issue is whether they undermine the foundation of our governmental system. When the federal government acts over and over again in ways that drain power away from the states toward the national government, it is time to reassess the process by which those actions are being taken.

NO. It is not a good idea to return power to the states in some misguided effort to regain some balance of power within the federal system. Certainly it is true that there have been power shifts away from the states and toward the national government, but those shifts have resulted in a nation that is far more respectful of human rights, much more interested in equality, and better governed than it would otherwise be.

First, it is noteworthy that the national government has used its power to come to grips with many violations of human rights perpetrated by state officials. As a result of federal legislation and court decisions, every level of government has become fairer and more equitable in dealing with citizens. The chapter essay reminds the reader that, in 1787, Americans were fearful of a large, powerful national government that might usurp or run roughshod over our rights. The irony is that it has been the states that have compiled a terrible record of rights abuses. In the area of criminal justice, for example, it took rulings from the U.S. Supreme Court to set down fair rules for the collection and use of evidence, the treatment of incarcerated persons, and the imposition of the death penalty. Indeed, the federal government waited decades to see if the states would mend their ways. When the states did not fix the problems, the federal government stepped into the arena in the 1960s and 1970s.

The most glaring examples of mistreatment by the states are in denial of civil rights of African-Americans. It was, after all, state laws that mandated separate schools, bathrooms, hospitals, courtroom Bibles, morgues, parks, theaters, sports arenas, train cars, and every other kind of public facility. Who knows how long it might have taken for states to enact laws ending segregation. Additionally, had it been left up to the states to end segregation, there would have been varying types and levels of enforcement as well. With just one sweep of the legislative hand, the federal government made most types of segregation illegal, with the same penalties nationwide for those who failed to comply. Clearly, the goal of equal treatment of citizens outweighs any theoretical benefit concerning federalism.

Those who want to reduce federal power and return various kinds of programs to the states argue that the federal government has used devious ways such as financial incentives, both positive and negative, and resorted to unfunded mandates to achieve its will. Rather than seeing these actions as harmful to federalism, one could just as easily view them as the mechanical means by which the national will is achieved. We should not forget that the legislation making segregated public facilities illegal was based on the Constitution's commerce clause. When it was challenged in court, the Supreme Court ruled the legislation constitutional.

Greater fairness is not limited to civil rights, either. Federal programs have also helped to even out disparities of resources, as some states are wealthier than others. Some, like Texas and California, have large numbers of immigrants and need to provide more services. Florida and Arizona have large numbers of elderly Americans, which means higher costs for programs geared toward that population. There is no reason why states should have to manage every problem on their own, without federal help. Federal programs allow resources to be directed where they are needed; the result is that disparities of resources, while still present, are less severe than they would be otherwise.

Finally, federal policies are often necessary because it is important that there be one policy instead of fifty. Thanks to technology, we are much closer to one another than we were when our Constitution was written. There can be no justification for differences in citizen rights from one state to another when our population is so mobile. There are also practical issues that necessitate states having the same policies. Take the issue of underage drinking. When each state decided its own drinking age without prodding from the federal government, the drinking age was routinely set at eighteen. Data clearly indicated that alcohol-related accidents, injuries and fatalities were high among persons in the 18-21 age group. Without federal incentives, some states might have raised their drinking age anyway while others might not have. Laws of that type would have encouraged young people to drive across state borders to drink where it was legal---and to drive back home under the influence of alcohol. This is not mere supposition. Since Louisiana resisted raising its drinking age, many young Texans traveled to Louisiana to drink legally. There were accidents and fatalities as a result when they tried to make their way home. This is just one example of why policy across the nation needs to be the same.

Federal officials have exercised wisdom in finding ways to have national policies even when the rules of federalism would seem to discourage them. Perhaps it is time to acknowledge that our needs now are generally for national policies, not local ones.

EXERCISE 4-2
Graphing the Federal Revenue Sharing Trend

Using the data provided in the table in Exercise 4-1, use the space below to draw a graph depicting the trend of federal funds as a percentage of revenues in Texas.

34% _____

32% _____

30% _____

28% _____

26% _____

24% _____

22% _____

20% _____

18% _____

78 79 80 81 82 83 84 85 86 87 88 89 90 91 92 93 94 95 96 97 98 99 00 01 02 03 04

Name		Seat	Score

EXERCISE 4-3
Your Philosophy of Government

Now that you have read the Pro & Con essay, apply what you have learned about federalism by reading the statement below and responding to it as requested.

Statement: Many people believe that one function that is local in nature and should remain so is operation of the public school system. They believe that only the local community can make effective decisions about what and how children should be taught. Others contend that the idea that education is local is outdated. Take a position on this issue (it need not coincide with your personal beliefs) and in the spaces below support the position you adopted with three arguments. Remember, opinion is not enough, so support your ideas with careful reasoning and facts wherever appropriate.

Position you will be defending on this issue:

_____

_____

Your supporting arguments:

1. _____

   _____

2. _____

   _____

3. _____

   _____

Now that you have given consideration to the question of whether public education should be a local activity, what are two other areas of government that you believe can best be handled locally? Identify two areas and briefly explain your reasoning.

1. _____

   _____

2. _____

   _____

Name	Seat	Score

CITY OF BOERNE, TEXAS v. FLORES, ARCHBISHOP OF SAN ANTONIO
June 25, 1997

An interesting court case that brings together issues of federalism and religious freedom is *City of Boerne (Texas) v. Flores*. St. Peter Catholic Church in Boerne, which is near San Antonio, Texas, was built in 1923 in the mission style and was designed to seat only about 230 people. Because the Church needed more space, the Archbishop's office filed applications with the City of Boerne for permits to add on to its building.

Invoking its zoning laws, the city denied the Church the permits because of the historic nature of the neighborhood in which it is located. City officials took the position that adding on to the Church building would unfavorably alter the beauty of the area. Upon receiving the city's decision, the Archbishop, acting on behalf of the Church, filed suit against Boerne, alleging that the city's action had violated the Religious Freedom Restoration Act (RFRA).

The Religious Freedom Restoration Act was a new law, having been enacted by Congress in 1993 in response to a ruling of the Supreme Court, *Employment Division, Department of Human Resources of Oregon v. Smith*. In that case, decided in 1991, the Supreme Court had ruled that Native Americans were not exempt from drug laws and therefore did not have the right to use peyote, a plant with hallucinogenic qualities, in their practice of religion. Because the use of peyote is a long-established practice, many people were shocked and upset that the Supreme Court did not uphold its use as lawful and protected.

As a result of the Supreme Court's ruling, the dismissal of two employees and the subsequent denial of unemployment benefits to them were upheld, because they had tested positive for the drug. In response to the Supreme Court's ruling, many members of Congress, including both Democrats and Republicans, wanted to enact legislation that would make it difficult for any level of government to interfere with any person's exercise of religion. The result was the Religious Freedom Restoration Act. Those acting on behalf of St. Peter Catholic Church in Boerne used the guarantees provided in RFRA to argue that the City of Boerne had no legal basis for denying the Church the building permits it had sought. To deny the permits, said the suit, was to infringe on religious freedom.

In the *Boerne* case, the Supreme Court held that the case "call[ed] into question the authority of Congress to enact RFRA" and to conclude that "the statute exceeds Congress' power." The Court viewed RFRA as an infringement on the power of states and localities by putting religion in a dominant position over government.

The public was split over the ruling, with many disagreeing and many others agreeing with the Supreme Court's action in overturning the Religious Freedom Restoration Act. This case and the court's ruling are important and interesting on a number of dimensions, including federalism. If you find this and related topics interesting, you may want to investigate these cases in greater detail. It is easy to find Supreme Court opinions on the Internet.

EXERCISE 4-4
Analyzing the *Boerne* Case

Please read the information on the preceding page before attempting to answer the questions below.

1.   Why do cities have zoning laws?

_____

_____

2.   Provide two examples of how a city might use its zoning laws to protect the residents of the city.

   a.   _____

   b.   _____

3.   Is it common or unusual for governments in the United States to interfere with the practice of religion? Take a position and explain your answer, providing examples as appropriate. (In addition to your own knowledge, you may need to consult the Internet for additional information.)

_____

_____

_____

4.   Do you think the Supreme Court ruled correctly in the *Boerne* case? Why or why not?

_____

_____

_____

_____

_____

Name		Seat	Score

CIVIL LIBERTIES IN THE UNITED STATES: DEMOCRACY AND THE WAR ON TERRORISM
Gloria C. Cox

During one of our last conversations, the late Supreme Court Justice William Brennan said, *"Look, pal, we've always known---the Framers knew---that liberty is a fragile thing."*(Nat Hentoff)

An immutable characteristic of our nation is freedom. If we allow the interests of "national security" to take away our freedoms, we surrender what it is to be an American. (American Civil Liberties Union)

A nation with many fears has taken steps to enhance its national security. New legislation allows government officials to keep track of who has crossed its borders and what they are doing while there. These new laws also permit greater surveillance of the citizenry in hopes of finding out who may be planning an attack. In addition, policies have been changed to allow authorities to put people in jail without charging them with a crime or even to deport them on many types of charges. Sound like a scary place to live? Well, it isn't China, Iran, Saudi Arabia, or other nations often associated with a deep sense of national paranoia. It is the United States since the terrorist attacks of September 11, 2001.

In every society there is a mix of freedom and order. Some degree of order is necessary if people are to go about their lives without undue fear. In a state of constant fear, progress would be impossible; in fact, many people would be so overcome by fear and insecurity that they would be unable to go to work or school, engage in recreational activities, or take care of their ordinary responsibilities.

Governments disagree on the appropriate level of order, of course. Some emphasize order by creating national police forces and powerful military establishments to control their population. Officials in such nations govern by instilling fear in the people. Police and other officials act in arbitrary and capricious ways, imprisoning and executing people and violating their most basic rights in other ways. You can probably think of several nations whose powerful dictators and state police control the apparatus of life and death for people.

Democratic nations, on the other hand, attempt to find a balance of order and freedom that will allow people to feel secure yet also free. They strive to find the level of order that allows people to go to school or work with the sense that they will be safe. However, the measures taken to bring about security should not violate the constitution or unduly burden the citizenry.

Unfortunately, even in democracies, periods of stress, such as when a nation experiences a terrible natural disaster, suffers an attack, or engages in a war, can motivate public officials to levy new restrictions in the hope of creating more security. In 2001, the United States experienced a terrible day of terrorist attacks, and, as a result, Americans have been forced to rethink the balance of freedom and order. Officials have promulgated new policies and created new restrictions on Americans. They have tightened the reins on information about government and what it is doing. This is the brave new world of America. Are Americans safer than before and just less free? This is the question to be explored in this essay.

Americans Times of Stress: Targeting Our Perceived Enemies

The terrorist attack of September 11, 2001, and the days and weeks following were not the first time our nation has experienced attacks deemed to strike at the heart of our existence as a nation. In the first part of this essay, we will briefly examine five particular times of national stress and how the United States responded to them.

Targeting our Perceived Enemies:
The Adams Administration

Our second President, John Adams, worried about the security of the young nation, and he convinced the Federalist Congress to adopt an Alien Enemies Act that "empowered the president in time of war to arrest, imprison, or banish the subjects of any hostile nation without specifying charges against them or providing opportunity for appeal" (Nash et al., 254). That law had the effect of suspending the Constitution for non-citizens, which is truly a shocking concept in a democracy. Adams also signed a Sedition Act entitled "An Act for the Punishment of Certain Crimes Against the United States." The Sedition Act of 1798 provided

> That if any person shall write, print, utter or publish, or shall cause or procure to be written, printed, uttered or published, or shall knowingly and willingly assist or aid in writing, printing, uttering, or publishing any false, scandalous, and malicious writings against the government of the United States, or either house of the Congress of the United States, or the President of the United States, such person...shall be punished by a fine...and by imprisonment (Yale).

Many people find it hard to believe that we ever had such laws, as they so clearly contradict the letter and spirit of the First Amendment. Yet our president and Congress saw them as necessary to prevent dissent against the government. And yes, the laws were actually used to charge, convict, and imprison people, who remained in prison until a new Congress and president repealed the legislation.

Targeting our Perceived Enemies:
Civil War and Martial Law

In a period of great national stress, martial law might be imposed. That would mean that our civil liberties are suspended and the military takes over enforcement of order, including the arrest and trial of civilians. It may surprise you to learn that martial law has been imposed in the United States on several occasions, although only in limited areas rather than throughout the nation. General Andrew Jackson imposed it in the area of New Orleans during the War of 1812. On three other occasions, martial law was declared in the area of a labor strike. San Francisco came under martial law following the 1906 earthquake, as did Hawaii following the Japanese attack on Pearl Harbor in December, 1941.

President Lincoln imposed martial law on certain areas and persons on September 15, 1863, during the Civil War. The actions Lincoln took were appealed to the Supreme Court by one person who, during martial law, was arrested and

tried by the military, then sentenced to death. In the case of *Ex Parte Milligan*, the Supreme Court ruled for Milligan and against martial law saying, "*Martial law...destroys every guarantee of the Constitution.*" By the time of the Court's decision, though, the Civil War had ended and Lincoln was dead of an assassin's bullet.

Targeting our Perceived Enemies:
The Effects of World War I

During and after World War I, one of the greatest concerns to American officials was the rise of Communism in Russia. Aliens in the United States were targeted for their sympathy with communist and other radical ideas. The attorney general, A. Mitchell Palmer, was the leader of a movement to rid the country of such elements, and he had some 6,000 aliens rounded up and imprisoned. Most were from European nations, and they held what was perceived as radical views on issues. No charges were brought against them, and most of them were eventually released, but not before they had endured a terrible experience that deprived them of civil rights guaranteed under the U.S. Constitution (Unger, 684-5).

Attorney General Palmer took a very hard line against aliens and communism, perceiving both to be enemies of the nation. He criticized others who did not share his opinions, and his words provide a key to his thinking about the dangers the nation faced:

> Like a prairie-fire, the blaze of revolution was sweeping over every American institution of law and order a year ago. It was eating its way into the homes of American workmen, its sharp tongues of revolutionary heat were licking the altars of the churches, leaping into the belfry of the school bell, crawling into the sacred corners of American homes, seeking to replace marriage vows with libertine laws, burning up the foundations of society (Palmer).

Much has been written about Palmer's actions, so you may want to investigate the subject further if you find it interesting.

Targeting our Perceived Enemies:
World War II

During World War II in the 1940s, the United States once again targeted its perceived enemies by requiring that immigrant Japanese and Japanese-Americans be moved from their homes on the West Coast to internment camps in the interior of the country. Approximately 120,000 men, women, and children were removed to inland areas, forced to leave behind their homes, land, possessions, and even their pets. About two-thirds of those treated in this way were American citizens.

This episode in our history is now well known, and during the 1980s, Congress and the President acted to provide remuneration for victims of those forced removals from place and property. Among the Americans who demanded internment of the Issei and Nisei was Earl Warren, later a champion of rights as Chief Justice of the United States (Unger, 747).

Targeting our Perceived Enemies:
The Cold War

The legacy of the Second World War was the Cold War, which pitted the two superpowers, the United States and the Soviet Union, against each other in a state of hostility and mistrust for several decades. Immediately after the end of World War II, there were more fears about Communist sympathizers in the United States, and Hollywood was supposedly the home of many of them. Many members of the entertainment industry were called to testify before Congressional committees, not only about their views but also about what they knew of others. Some cooperated yet others refused and even went into exile to escape the scrutiny. Many were blacklisted and did not work again in Hollywood.

The record of the infamous House Committee on Un-American Activities (HUAC), which boasted Richard Nixon as a member, provided an indicator of the times. The Senate, too, had its own self-appointed Communist hunter in the person of Joseph McCarthy. This man became well known for announcing that there were Communists everywhere in government, from the U.S. Army to the State Department. President Eisenhower stood up to McCarthy by denying him the Army records he sought in his bid to ruin as many military careers as he could. The Senate finally grew tired of McCarthy's tactics and censured him, thus ending his hurtful campaign.

Since September 11, 2001

September 11, 2001 has taken its place as one of the saddest days in our national history, along with December 7, 1941, when the Japanese bombed Pearl Harbor, and November 22, 1963, when President Kennedy was murdered. We are still dealing with the aftermath of the terrorist attacks of September 11, 2001, and the changes in our society are profound. Is it too soon to see whether our responses have been appropriate or excessive, as they have sometimes been in the past? Are they achieving the goal of making us safer? The remainder of the essay explores how we have responded and what the implications of our responses are.

What Has the United States Done Since the Terrorist Attacks of September 11, 2001?

I.   The United States established the Department of Homeland Security.

One of the first steps President Bush took after the attacks was propose a new cabinet department, the Department of Homeland Security, to be headed by a Secretary of Homeland Security. The first person to hold the post was former New Jersey Governor Tom Ridge, who was confirmed in early 2003. Various agencies were moved into the new department, including the Coast Guard, the Customs Service, the Immigration and Naturalization Service, and the Transportation Security Administration (Homeland Security). Responsibilities of the Immigration and Naturalization Service were transferred to a new agency, the U.S. Citizenship and Immigration Services (USCIS). Enforcement of immigration laws, customs laws, and air security laws were put together in another new agency, Immigration and Customs Enforcement, known as I.C.E. (Homeland Security). Clearly, it is too early to assess the effectiveness of such a large new cabinet department, but there has been some early criticism as the Department took controversial steps. Harpers Magazine provided several examples, all gleaned from other sources cited in the article, including the following:

- When Texas Democratic legislators left the State in 2003 to deprive Republicans of a quorum for a vote on reapportionment, the Department of Homeland Security was enlisted to track them down.

- In 2004, the Department decided that tougher restrictions would be placed on visitors to the United States from Britain, France, Australia, and other nations. Visitors have not taken kindly to the requirements for photographs and fingerprints, and U.S. visitors have experienced retaliation by some of the affected nations.

- In 2004, it was revealed that the Census Bureau was supplying the Department with information about Arab-Americans, including zip codes, adding additional concerns about racial profiling to those already circulating.

Regardless of these situations which some will perceive as inappropriate, the Department of Homeland Security is a large department charged with significant responsibilities. It will be important to continue assessing its progress in confronting security issues for the United States.

II.   The United States enacted the USA PATRIOT Act.

The other key piece of the government's strategy is the USA PATRIOT Act, which is an acronym for the Uniting and Strengthening America by Providing Appropriate Tools Required to Intercept and Obstruct Terrorism Act of 2001. It was enacted in October, 2001 at the urging of then-Attorney General John Ashcroft, who went on a nationwide tour to promote the legislation. According to the American Civil Liberties Union, Ashcroft asserted in Congressional testimony that "anyone who raised concerns about his actions would 'aid terrorists' and 'give ammunition to America's enemies' " (ACLU).

The USA PATRIOT Act proved to be a popular proposal with Members of Congress; the Senate approved it 98-1 and the House voted in favor by a margin of 356-66 (ABC News). However, it is a law that has many people across the country wondering what the impact on civil liberties will be because it authorizes sweeping new powers for the executive branch.

One new power allows the federal government to require men from several nations that are considered supporters of terrorism to report for interviews with officials of the Immigration and Naturalization Service. Some men have complied, although some have been arrested and deported when they sought to comply with the requirement (CNN.com). The

actions taken with regard to such persons are subject to "little or no judicial review" (Herman). This detention of persons has created considerable concern, as we do not know how many are being detained, the extent or quality of the evidence against them, or the conditions under which they are being kept (Herman).

Additionally, then-Attorney General John Ashcroft announced that when persons suspected of involvement with terrorism are jailed, they will no longer have a private attorney-client relationship, as "he intends to eavesdrop on inmates' attorney-client conversations." Moreover, many Americans have been interviewed by federal agents, their having been selected apparently on the basis of their ethnicity and/or their religion (Herman).

Beyond provisions dealing with aliens, the law contains several other important changes to federal law, which are briefly summarized here:

1. The law gives federal authorities important new powers allowing access to communications in order to check for terrorist or other criminal threats.

2. It increases the power of law enforcement authorities to deal with money laundering.

3. It tightens U.S. borders and imposes new rules on non-citizens in the United States.

4. It "creates new crimes, new penalties, and new procedural efficiencies for use against domestic and international terrorists" (Doyle).

There are two views of the PATRIOT Act. Many see the law as an extremely important step in the nation's fight against terrorism. They believe that federal authorities need enhanced powers to deal with a foe that is like no other this nation has ever seen. On the other side, many believe that the PATRIOT Act represents a terrible encroachment on civil liberties without providing any new security for the United States.

The American Civil Liberties Union is one among many organizations to voice disagreement with its provisions. Laura W. Murphy, Director of the ACLU's Washington National Office, said that "The [USA PATRIOT] Act is based on the faulty assumption that safety must come at the expense of civil liberties." Some cities around the United States have expressed by nonbinding resolution their opposition to the expansion of federal powers in certain areas under the law. Among those is the city of Cambridge, Massachusetts, whose city council said, "We believe these civil liberties.... are now threatened by the USA PATRIOT Act" (Schabner). However, Mark Corallo, Justice Department spokesman, said that the "USA PATRIOT Act was passed by an overwhelming bipartisan majority in both the House and the Senate. The PATRIOT Act protects civil liberties and is fully within the bounds of the Constitution."

In February, 2003, there were leaks of a new draft law called the Domestic Security Enhancement Act of 2003, dubbed PATRIOT Act II, which has not yet been sent to Congress for consideration. According to the draft available on the Internet, the Freedom of Information Act would be altered to further restrict citizen access to government information. The law would also allow state and local law enforcement agencies to spy on Americans, lifting agreements made in the past to disallow such surveillance. Also included in the law is a provision to strip citizenship from any person who "gives 'material support' to any group that the attorney general designates as a terrorist organization" (Balkin). Among the other provisions of the law (which number in excess of 100) are new powers for government officials to collect DNA from suspected terrorists, get credit reports on individuals, and allow for the prosecution of a government official who reveals the existence of a terrorist investigation (OMB Watcher). It remains to be seen if this proposal will be submitted to Congress and whether Congress will give its approval.

III.   Other Important Policy Changes

Creation of the new Department of Homeland Security and passage of the USA PATRIOT Act are not the only actions taken by federal officials to increase our security. Many changes have been instituted, and some of them may even affect you.

Greater Government Secrecy

The U.S. government collects and maintains large amounts of information on all sorts of things, ranging from data on natural resources to personal information about every American. Since the 1960s, the policy has been to make available to the public as much information as possible on things--reactors, dams, water supplies, agriculture, and so on--while protecting personal data about people. In fact, agencies of government were prohibited from even merging files in order to prevent the creation of dossiers on individual citizens.

Since September 11, 2001, two things have happened in the government's handling of information. The first thing is that we no longer have access to a great deal of information that was available until that fateful day. Immediately following the attacks, Internet sites were changed and much data was removed. The reasoning was that if Americans could get the information, so could America's enemies. New York, a state with reason for wariness, went even further than the federal government by ruling that anything deemed "sensitive information" would be withheld (Graham).

At the same time, we as individuals have fewer rights relative to the private information government agencies have about us. As a result of the USA PATRIOT Act, the Federal Bureau of Investigation and other law enforcement agencies are finding it easier to get personal information about us, including "business records, medical records, educational records, and library records" (American Library Association). According to Harpers Magazine, "Attorney General John Ashcroft mocked librarians for their opposition to provisions of the USA PATRIOT Act that permit federal agencies to seize library records."

Government officials would argue, of course, that without information at their disposal, it is impossible to identify threats or potential threats against the security of the United States. Those opposed to the law would argue that information is power, and our civil liberties are at risk when agents of the government have access to it. Whichever side you favor in this argument, you will still no doubt regard these issues as very important.

Restrictions on foreign students wishing to enter the United States

Students from other nations are a matter of concern for the U.S. officials. A new online tracking system has been established, and colleges and universities are required to use it to enter information about foreign students studying on their campus. The system is known as SEVIS, which stands for Student and Exchange Visa Information Service (CNN.Com, January 2003). The tracking system was actually approved several years ago, but colleges and universities generally opposed it, so it had not been implemented. The USA PATRIOT Act required its immediate implementation. Universities must supply information about foreign students or face major penalties, up to and including not being allowed to enroll foreign students at the institution (SEVIS.net).

SEVIS kicks in once students are actually enrolled at American universities, but for many foreign students, the initial hurdle is getting approval to enter the United States. Officials say that they have "intensified scrutiny" of foreign students seeking visas to enter the United States (Walfish, A40).

Additionally, universities must also cooperate with the Federal Bureau of Investigation when FBI officials request information about foreign students. Recent news articles suggest that the FBI is actually working with campus police forces to secure access to information about foreign students. The FBI and the Department of Justice say that, because of the PATRIOT Act, institutions can supply the data the FBI wants without notifying the students who are involved. The Department of Education has expressed concern about the practice and has taken the position that institutions should not be required to supply such information (Eggen).

How Will These Actions Affect Our Civil Liberties?

It has been a relatively short time since the terrorist attacks against the United States, so it is far too soon to know how effective the steps our government has taken will be in deterring future attacks on the United States. It is also too soon to determine the effect of these various measures on our civil liberties. We do recognize, though, our history of responding to threats with curbs on civil liberties and special treatment of aliens in the United States.

At this time, many people and organizations, both liberal and conservative, are expressing concern about the direction in which the United States is headed. The American Civil Liberties Union has been calling attention to the greater surveillance to which we are all exposed these days. Bob Barr, a former member of Congress from Georgia and well-known conservative, remarked, "That sphere of what's left of privacy gets smaller and smaller and smaller. Each incremental taking away of that privacy by the government becomes much more important" (CBS News, May 15, 2002).

If our government goes ahead with new, heretofore unimagined limits on the civil liberties of Americans, all certainly done in an effort to make us more secure, have we lost, perhaps forever, the liberty that made us the nation we are? Will the first years of the twenty-first century be seen later as the era when we destroyed the nation to save it? It is a hard question, but one that is greatly deserving of our consideration.

PRO & CON
It's the Twenty-first Century:
Should We Still Have the Death Penalty?

YES, even though we have arrived at the twenty-first century, there is still a need for the death penalty in the United States. Just ask any of the thousands of persons who are mourning the loss of a spouse, child, or other family member through violent crime.

Recall the discussion of order and its importance from the previous essay. If society is to function effectively, it is imperative that laws be enforced and that a certain level of order be maintained. Take the recent news of two little girls having been murdered in Florida. In separate incidents, the girls were abducted, each by a different sex offender, then assaulted and murdered. What should be done to people who carry out such heinous crimes against little children? Or take another example: a few years ago, the Washington, D.C., Maryland, and Virginia area was terrorized by a sniper who randomly killed people who were shopping, driving, or filling their cars with gasoline. People were terrified to carry out their normal daily activities. What kind of punishment is appropriate for a person who uses a high-powered rifle to pick off victim after victim and create such an atmosphere of fear? Sadly, we live in a society where terrible crimes are still all-too-common. Does anyone really need to be reminded of the murders committed by Jeffrey Dahmer, Ted Bundy, Wayne Gacy, or other serial killers? Can anyone truly make an argument that our society would somehow be improved by allowing these criminals to live?

The death penalty has long been used as a method of keeping order. The Code of Hammaurabi of Ancient Babylon in the eighteenth century B.C.E. contained the death penalty for 25 different crimes. The Draconian Code of Ancient Athens, which dates from the seventh century B.C.E., prescribed death as the penalty for all crimes. There were many forms of execution, including drowning, crucifixion, beating the offender to death or burning him alive, and impalement. By the tenth century C.E., hanging was the usual method (Death Penalty Information Center).

The death penalty has always been a part of American society, even from the earliest colonial days. The first execution was in 1608, but we also know that by 1612, the death penalty was provided for crimes such as stealing grapes or chickens, or trading with Native Americans (Death Penalty Information Center).

Today, of course, states cannot impose the death penalty except for the crime of murder, the taking of the life of another person. Following the challenge to the death penalty in the 1970s, state legislatures enacted legislation spelling out exactly which crimes are capital crimes, i.e., those that could result in the death penalty. At the same time, elaborate safeguards were initiated to make sure that only those who are truly guilty are assessed the ultimate penalty.

On January 1, 2005, there were 3,455 men and women on death row in prisons across the United States. Texas had 447 men and women on death row awaiting execution by lethal injection. Only California with 639 had more prisoners than Texas under a sentence of death. Since the death penalty was reinstated in 1976, Texas has executed 340 people. During the same time period, eight persons have been freed from death row in Texas, having been found innocent, and two others were granted clemency (Death Penalty Information Center).

Although the state is often criticized for the large number of executions it carries out, the crimes for which one can be sentenced to death are very clear. They include murder of a law enforcement officer; murder during the commission of another felony; multiple murders; murder for hire; and murder of a child (Court Online). Clearly this is not a penalty that is lightly imposed on anyone.

NO, the death penalty is no longer defensible. In early 2003, outgoing Governor of Illinois George H. Ryan made a courageous decision to commute the sentences of those on death row to life in prison. He took that step because he believed there was reasonable doubt about the guilt of some of those persons. Illinois had executed 12 people, but 13 others sentenced to die had been set free because they were found to be innocent (National Coalition). Governor Ryan understood that no civil liberty is more important than the right to life. Of the many reasons why the death penalty should be abolished, I will discuss just three in this essay. They should be sufficient to cause the United States to end the death penalty.

First, the death penalty is based on the premise that the justice system never errs. Once the death penalty is carried out, there is no going back because the person is dead. There are those who say that the system has so many safeguards that no innocent person could ever reach the death chamber, but we know otherwise. In Texas, lawyers representing those on trial for their life have actually slept through testimony. That means there could be many people on death row in Texas who are innocent. Illinois acknowledged that fact for its system, so we in Texas need to recognize that possibility, too. It is foolish to argue that mistakes are never made and that safeguards are sufficient.

Second, the death penalty is a shocking event that dehumanizes and degrades us. We often hear the argument that some crimes are so heinous that only the death penalty can atone for the act. There is no doubt that brutal, unspeakable crimes are committed, but to carry out the death penalty requires the state to engage in a cold-blooded act that mobilizes the machinery of medicine. Officials take a living person into a room and remove from it a dead person.

Finally, the death penalty has separated the United States from other nations in the developed world and placed us in the company of nations whose human rights records are at a much lower standard than ours, except when it comes to the death penalty. It is a matter of concern when our human rights policies are the same, at least on this count, as that of China, Saudi Arabia, or Yemen. This point is well illustrated by comments on behalf of Amnesty International, an organization that is fighting to end the death penalty. In Amnesty's view, "The death penalty is the ultimate denial of human rights. It is the premeditated and cold-blooded killing of a human being by the state in the name of justice. It violates the right to life as proclaimed in the Universal Declaration of Human Rights" (Amnesty International). If the United States wishes to have a moral and ethical voice in world affairs, it will have to join with the other civilized nations that have abandoned the death penalty.

EXERCISE 5-1
The Death Penalty

As you live and study in a state that employs the death penalty, it is appropriate to investigate the use of the ultimate punishment. Please answer the questions below by researching the topic. Internet sites you may wish to investigate are Amnesty International at www.amnesty.usa and the Death Penalty Information Center at www.deathpenaltyinfo.org

1. _____ How many states have the death penalty?

2. _____ How many people are on death row in the United States? (Be sure to look up the current figure.)

3. _____ How many people are on death row in Texas? (Be sure to look up the current figure.)

4. What is the racial mix of Texas death row inmates? In the second set of blanks, note the percentage of the Texas population constituted by each particular group.
    _____ Whites   _____ Whites
    _____ Blacks   _____ Blacks
    _____ Hispanics   _____ Hispanics

5. What is the judicial process for imposing the death penalty in Texas?

    _____

    _____

6. What rule does Texas have with regard to victims' families viewing an execution?

    _____

    _____

7. In the essay you have just read, with arguments for and against the death penalty, what do you think is the least convincing argument, and why?

    _____

    _____

    _____

Name		Seat	Score

EXERCISE 5-2
Executing Juvenile Offenders

In 2005, the U.S. Supreme Court ruled in *Roper v. Simmons* that it is unconstitutional to execute offenders who were not yet 18 years old when they committed the crime for which they are being sentenced.

1. What was the vote in the Supreme Court and which justices voted on each side of the issue?

    _____

    _____

    _____

2. _____ How many inmates in the United States were affected by the ruling?

    _____ How many inmates in Texas were affected by the ruling?

3. Courts in the State of Missouri, where the *Roper* case originated, said that a national consensus has developed in the United States against executing persons who were juveniles when they committed their crime. Explain why you agree or disagree with the view that a national consensus exists on this issue.

    _____

    _____

    _____

4. Justice Anthony Kennedy wrote in the majority opinion, "The age of 18 is the point where society draws the line for many purposes between childhood and adulthood. It is, we conclude, the age at which the line for death penalty eligibility ought to rest." Agree or disagree with Justice Kennedy and explain your reasoning in the space provided.

    _____

    _____

    _____

5. What happened to prisoners in Texas who were affected by the ruling?

    _____

    _____

    _____

Name		Seat	Score

EXERCISE 5-3
Banning Books

One of the important rights guaranteed by the First Amendment is the right to read what others have written, whether it is a flier, a newspaper, a magazine, or a book. In fact, few things are more important than books, because they are windows to a world of ideas. Many people see them as dangerous, though, and would restrict their availability. The American Library Association website deals with the issue of banned books. Please visit the ALA web site to answer the questions below.

1. Mindful that children may lack the maturity or knowledge to deal with some subjects, we commonly accept the view that books on these subjects should be kept away from children until they reach a certain age. Identify three subjects you would keep away from children in each of the following age groups:

AGE GROUP	Subject #1	Subject #2	Subject #3
Under age 6			
Age 6-10			
Age 10-15			

2. From the American Library Association web site, list seven common reasons why books are banned.
    a. _____
    b. _____
    c. _____
    d. _____
    e. _____
    f. _____
    g. _____

3. Where are most books challenged?

    _____

4. Who is most likely to bring a protest?

    _____

5. Name ten people or groups who have attempted to ban books. Place an asterisk beside the one who is MOST likely to try to ban a book.

    _____   _____

    _____   _____

    _____   _____

    _____   _____

    _____   _____

6.   List ten books that are on the most banned list.

   _____

   _____

   _____

   _____

   _____

   _____

   _____

   _____

   _____

   _____

7.   Now, take a look at your list or the entire list on the web site and locate a book that you have read. Use the space below to agree or disagree with banning the book. Be sure to mention at what age, if any, the book would be appropriate. If you can't locate a book you have read, pick one from the list and research it a bit as to why some people view it as objectionable.

   Name of Book   _____

   _____

   _____

   _____

   _____

Name	Seat	Score

EXERCISE 5-4
Cohen v. California, 403 U.S. 15 (1971)

One of the fundamental rights guaranteed by the First Amendment is the right to express our ideas and opinions. Of course, not all expressions of ideas and opinions are actually speeches. Instead, expression may be a sign you carry in a demonstration or even a flag you burn. This exercise is designed to acquaint you with an interesting and important case that advanced the cause of free speech.

To answer the questions below, you will need to find a copy of the Supreme Court's ruling in the case of *Cohen v. California,* 1971. You may use the Internet, such as Findlaw.com, you may consult a constitutional law book, or you may research the case in the government documents section of the library.

1.   What did Mr. Cohen do that upset authorities?

_____

_____

2.   Explain what you think Cohen's attitude was. Did he intend to make a scene or cause a disturbance?

_____

_____

3.   Was Cohen's message a political one? Why?

_____

_____

4.   What circumstances caused this case to be an important one?

_____

_____

5.   What was the Supreme Court's ruling in the case?

_____

_____

6. Identify and explain three major legal issues that constitute the heart of the Supreme Court's ruling in *Cohen v. California*. You will need to read Justice Harlan's opinion to find these points of law.

   a. _____

   _____

   b. _____

   _____

   c. _____

   _____

7. The statement below appears in Justice Harlan's opinion. Please use the space below to analyze this statement, explain what it means, and demonstrate why it is important. Include some contemporary examples that illustrate the ideas contained in the statement.

   "…while the particular four-letter word being litigated here is perhaps more distasteful than most others of its genre, it is nevertheless often true that one man's vulgarity is another's lyric."

   _____

   _____

   _____

   _____

   _____

   _____

   _____

   _____

   _____

   _____

Name		Seat	Score

EXERCISE 5-5
Chapter Review

Please select the best answer to each question below and write your answer in the blank provided. Answers to all questions can be found in the chapter essay and Pro & Con article.

1. _____ At times of threats to our security, we have tended to
    A. act with care and deliberation so as not to worsen the situation.
    B. give government officials greater power to restrict civil liberties.
    C. act internationally with no change in domestic policy.
    D. rely on our allies for assistance.

2. _____ President John Adams saw the usefulness of laws to
    A. choke off speech and debate about political issues and public figures.
    B. maximize the freedom enjoyed by the American people.
    C. hold government officials accountable for their behavior.
    D. help the young nation build alliances with friendly nations abroad.

3. _____ When martial law is declared,
    A   our civil liberties are suspended.
    B. the military assumes power to enforce order.
    C. even civilians may be tried in military courts.
    D. all of the answers above are correct.
    E. none of the answers above is correct.

4. _____ Martial law has
    A. never been declared in the United States.
    B. been declared only once---during the Civil War.
    C. been declared on many occasions that are simply too numerous to count.
    D. been declared on several occasions in specific areas, usually after a natural disaster or incident of labor unrest.

5. _____ Concerning President Lincoln's actions during the Civil War, the Supreme Court ruled that
    A. The president's power during wartime is unlimited.
    B. No president can declare martial law, regardless of the situation.
    C. Lincoln should have gotten Congressional approval for his actions.
    D. Lincoln's actions were not lawful.

6. _____ In the United States, in 1918 when World War I ended
    A. Large numbers of Americans embraced Communist ideology.
    B. The Depression consumed so much energy and attention that there was very little interest in political affairs.
    C. it was common for returning veterans to demonstrate and even riot violently over their inability to find jobs.
    D. Aliens were subject to mistreatment, often including imprisonment and deportation.

7. _____ Who was A. Mitchell Palmer?
   A. The first director of the F.B.I.
   B. U. S. Senator who accused many Americans of being communist sympathizers
   C. Attorney General who rounded up and imprisoned or deported many people
   D. The current attorney general of the United States

8. _____ Of the groups below, who did the United States target for internment in camps during World War II?
   A. Communists and those thought to be pro-Russian
   B. Jewish Americans
   C. Immigrant Japanese and Japanese Americans
   D. Immigrant Germans and German Americans

9. _____ The Department of _____ was established following the September 11, 2001, attacks.
   A. National Security   C. Homeland Security
   B. Security Protection   D. National Homeland Security

10. _____ The USA PATRIOT Act
   A. allows for greater surveillance activities by government officials.
   B. allows citizenship to be stripped from any person who aids terrorism.
   C. makes it illegal for foreign students to come to the United States.
   D. requires all aliens to be interviewed by the INS each year.

11. _____ What is SEVIS?
   A. A system to track the movement of aliens in the U.S.
   B. An agreement between the FBI and U.S. colleges and universities
   C. A system for keeping track of foreign students at U.S. colleges and universities
   D. A new legal system to be used in cases involving terrorist acts

12. _____ Which aspect of the USA PATRIOT Act is opposed by the American Library Association?
   A. The implementation of a federal list of banned books
   B. Access of federal agents to many records, including library records
   C. Establishment of a watch list of citizens who check out certain books
   D. Withdrawal of all government materials from library holdings

Name		Seat	Score

AN IMPORTANT ISSUE OF CIVIL RIGHTS:
AFFIRMATIVE ACTION IN HIGHER EDUCATION
Gloria C. Cox

"It is far too late to argue that the guarantee of equal protection to all persons permits the recognition of special wards entitled to a degree of protection greater than that accorded others." (Justice Powell in the case of *Regents of the University of California v. Bakke*, 1978.)

Over the past few decades, administrators and faculty have come to embrace diversity in higher education because of the opportunities it creates for teaching and learning. Ironically, during the same period, our ability to ensure that students and faculty of different racial and ethnic backgrounds can come to our institutions has become subject to more and more constraints. (Milem)

The Debate About Affirmative Action

Our society has made great progress in realizing its goal of equal opportunity for all Americans. Barriers that once stopped women and minorities from entering certain programs, institutions, or professions are now gone. Federal laws guard against discrimination in the work place, the education system, and the voting booth, offering recourse for those who experience discrimination.

A great many Americans believe that elimination of those barriers brought about equality of opportunity for women and African Americans. Other Americans believe that merely eliminating barriers is not enough because that does not help women, African Americans, or other minorities overcome the effects of past discrimination. They believe that catching up will require pro-active steps, or affirmative action, if minorities are to compete on a level playing field with white males who have not suffered hundreds of years of discrimination.

Isn't Discrimination Illegal Under Our Constitution?

Yes, since 1868, the Fourteenth Amendment has required states to provide equal protection for all residents, and that protection extends to the federal government through the Fifth Amendment. However, long after the Equal Protection Clause was part of the Constitution, many types of discrimination still existed. Discrimination on the basis of race was common in deciding who could vote, who would be hired or promoted, who would be admitted to college, and even who could eat at restaurants, attend plays and concerts, or be treated at a hospital. The civil rights movement of the 1950s and 1960s led

to passage of legislation and court rulings designed to end discrimination on the basis of race.

You may be wondering how affirmative action can be constitutional if all types of discrimination are against the law. Actually, there is a legal principle for categorizing people by race, but those who attempt to do so must assume a formidable legal burden. They must demonstrate to the satisfaction of the courts that what they are doing advances a *compelling national objective* that cannot be achieved in any other manner.

Affirmative action is based on the idea that it is not sufficient merely to eliminate past discrimination. Instead, positive steps must be taken to overcome the effects of all those years of discrimination. Universities have made the case, and the courts have agreed, that diversity in the student population and faculty is desirable. In the *Bakke* ruling in 1978, the Supreme Court established the acceptability of affirmative action in college admissions by saying that race can be one factor that colleges consider in their admissions policies, but that quota systems would not be acceptable (Springer, 2).

Affirmative action actually began in 1965 when President Lyndon Johnson promulgated executive order 11873. Affirmative action policies were established and implemented in higher education, employment, and government contracts. It has remained a controversial policy throughout the almost four decades of its history. The major arguments on each side of the controversy are provided below.

Arguments in favor of affirmative action
- Affirmative action was instituted to make up for past discrimination, which lasted

71

hundreds of years. We have not yet had affirmative action for a sufficient period of time to overcome the effects of so much discrimination.

- Affirmative action helps to diversify educational institutions as well as the workplace, which has positive effects on our society.
- Affirmative action has only increased opportunities for minorities, not hurt other groups such as white men. After all, most of the positions of power are still occupied by white men.
- Race-blind policies actually hurt minority students because white students have a great deal more educational opportunity to prepare them for college than minority students do.

Arguments against Affirmative Action

- We have had affirmative action in place for more than thirty-five years, which is a generation and then some. That should be enough time to even out the playing field so that everyone has equal opportunity.
- Our Constitution does not permit special treatment for any person, whether minority or not. We either have a fair legal system, or we do not.
- With laws in place to guarantee women and minorities equal educational opportunity, qualified students are admitted, as evidenced by the diverse environment of colleges and universities today.
- Affirmative action often becomes reverse discrimination, where qualified white males are turned away in favor of lesser qualified women and minorities. Such reverse discrimination creates anger and hostility, which may contribute to racial prejudice.

Each of these arguments could be the basis for a long and protracted debate, as many complex details and ideas are involved. However, it is not the purpose of this essay to attempt to discuss each idea and arrive at a conclusion. Rather, it is to see how a particular policy has evolved and how some states have made changes in affirmative action.

Affirmative Action and Higher Education

Much of the discussion and litigation surrounding affirmative action has centered on higher education. There are two main areas in higher education where affirmative action is important: hiring faculty members and admitting students. Suppose a university sets aside funds to offer special financial incentives to attract minority faculty members, and a minority male and a white male with the same credentials are hired by the same department at the same time. As a result of affirmative action efforts to attract minority faculty, the minority male starts with a substantially higher salary than the white male. Is that legal, or has the white instructor been the victim of discrimination? On this issue, the Nevada Supreme Court upheld the salary differential as justified in order to diversify the faculty of the university, whose faculty was just one percent minority (Springer).

The other big issue, the one about which we hear the most, is admissions policies. After all, most programs at universities have a limited number of spaces to be filled. Think of medical school, law school, and other programs that must select perhaps 100 or 200 students from a pool of 500 or more applicants. Those denied admission have sometimes gone to court, either to contend that the institution had policies in place that unfairly denied admission to minority applicants or that the university's policies to make sure that minority applicants were admitted unfairly denied admission to white applicants.

The best known such case is *Regents of the University of California v. Bakke*. It concerned an admissions program at the Medical School at the University of California in Davis, which operated two parallel admissions systems, one of them reserved for applicants who "were economically or educationally disadvantaged, or were black, Chicano, Asian, or Native American" (Epstein and Walker, 747). With this system in place, some minority applicants were admitted to medical school over white applicants with higher scores and grades. Bakke was a white male who believed he was better qualified than some minority candidates who were admitted, so he brought suit against the university. His case went all the way to the Supreme Court, which disallowed quotas but permitted race to be considered as one element of the admissions decision.

Almost everyone would agree that the Court's ruling in *Bakke* failed to provide the guidance and clarity on affirmative action that many college and university officials wanted (and needed), so debate has continued since the ruling. Over the years, the Supreme Court has considered a number of affirmative action cases, but the University of Michigan cases are the first cases dealing with higher education since *Bakke*.

In the years since the *Bakke* decision, most colleges and universities have practiced affirmative action in admissions, financial aid, and faculty employment decisions. They have done so not because they were required to by a court, but because of two underlying justifications (Springer, 2003).

- Affirmative action is an effective means of remedying the effects of past discrimination; and
- Affirmative action helps to create a diverse student body and university community, which is an important part of the educational experience

Over the years, support for affirmative action appears to have diminished. Several factors may help explain this decline. First, many Americans who are competing for college admission and job opportunities today do not remember the civil rights movements or the blatant forms of discrimination that it ended. Second, there is a large and growing African American middle class. Some take the position that our society has changed a great deal since affirmative action was inaugurated, and that the people most deserving of special help today are children from poor families regardless of their race. They argue that children of middle and upper middle class African American families enjoy opportunities that are comparable to those of white families, and those who really need affirmative action are poor children, whether they are minorities or not.

Finally, the national political climate for this issue has changed. Our presidents for more than two decades have been lukewarm toward affirmative action or even opposed to it. Of the last four presidents, only Mr. Clinton supported affirmative action. Even he acknowledged some problems with the system, as he called for it to be fixed rather than discarded. When the Supreme Court accepted two cases on affirmative action for review, President George W. Bush decided that the weight of the federal government would be thrown against affirmative action.

The Michigan Cases

During the 2002 term, the Supreme Court of the United States considered two important affirmative action cases from the University of Michigan. This event marked the first time in twenty-five years that the Supreme Court agreed to rule on an affirmative action issue involving institutions of higher education. College and university officials, as well as many others around the nation, hoped that the Court would use this opportunity to resolve many outstanding issues and unanswered questions about affirmative action.

One of the cases from the University of Michigan was filed in 1997 by two students who were refused admission to the University's undergraduate program (Schmidt and Selingo). The university was using a point system for determining undergraduate admissions, with applicants being awarded points for various aspects of their credentials. For example, an applicant with a perfect SAT score of 1600 would receive 12 points. If the student's essay was deemed excellent, the applicant would receive another 3 points (CNN). The maximum number of points that any applicant could receive was 150 points. Each minority student, and some lower socio-economic status students as well, received 20 points as part of their total. The plaintiffs argued that this admissions procedure worked against some non-minority students who did not receive the 20 point bonus. The Supreme Court had to decide whether this admissions procedure violated the equal protection clause of the Fourteenth Amendment, and therefore, the rights of some applicants.

The case was argued before the Supreme Court in April, 2003. One indicator of the importance of a case can be seen in the number of amicus curiae briefs filed by persons or groups on each side of the issue. Not surprisingly, these affirmative action cases elicited a large number of briefs. President Bush directed the Justice Department to file a brief in opposition to the university's admission policies and affirmative action. General Motors and Microsoft were among a large number of major corporations filing briefs supporting the position of the University of Michigan. In addition, a number of well-known retired military officers filed in support of affirmative action programs (CNN).

Changes in the States

When policies are undergoing a period of transition, we can often see the first changes taking place in states. In fact, challenges have caused limits to be placed on affirmative action in California, Louisiana, Mississippi, Florida, Maryland, Washington, Georgia, and Texas (Civil Rights Commission). In California, it was voters who in 1996 banned affirmative action by approving Proposition 209. The rule in California is that students who graduate in the top 4% of their high school classes will be admitted to the University of California System (Springer, 2003). Similarly, in November, 1998, voters in the State of Washington "passed an initiative banning race-conscious affirmative action in the public sector (Springer, 2003).

Another important example of changes in policy comes from Florida, where in 1999, Governor Jeb Bush "banned all use of affirmative action in admissions to state schools" (Springer, 2003). Governor Bush recommended the One Florida initiative that "guarantees admission at the state's public colleges and universities to the top 20% of graduating seniors from all Florida high schools" (Springer, 2003). According to the One Florida website, the Talented 20 Program requires that students have 19 academic credits and have taken the SAT or ACT. Students who qualify can gain admission to one of eleven universities and "are given priority for the awarding of funds from the Florida Student Assistance Grant, a needs-based program." One interesting part of the plan is free PSAT or PLAN testing for all 10th graders (web site). Since adoption of the One Florida plan, Florida officials have announced that minority enrollment is up at the University of Florida after two years of decline, and minority enrollment has held steady at other state institutions. Officials credit innovative recruitment programs and stepped-up recruitment efforts (Powers).

For those of us studying American and Texas government, the most interesting changes have come here in Texas, as the state has responded to the ruling of the Fifth Circuit Court of Appeals in the famous *Hopwood* case. That case began in 1992 when four white students, denied admission to the University of Texas Law School, filed suit in federal court, claiming they had been the victims of race discrimination. The case wound its way through the legal system, with the Fifth Circuit Court of Appeals eventually ruling that race-based policies are not constitutionally acceptable. The U.S. Supreme Court denied a petition to hear the case, which effectively ended the litigation. Texas Attorney General Dan Morales interpreted the *Hopwood* ruling as prohibiting the use of "race as a factor in admissions, financial aid or retention programs" (Lum, 1997).

Coming to terms with the *Hopwood* ruling is just one of the challenges facing higher education in Texas. In October, 2000, the Texas Higher Education Coordinating Board adopted a master plan entitled *Closing the Gaps* that sets goals for student participation, success, excellence, and research by 2015. State officials, including the legislature, signed on to the report and its goals in 2001. The report addresses a very serious problem that will, unless solved, have dire consequences for the state in a few decades. Texas has a smaller percentage of students attending college than other states. The purpose of *Closing the Gaps* is to increase the percentage of Texans in college.

Officials in Texas have recognized the seriousness of the situation the state faces by having a lower-than-average participation in higher education and have taken several important steps in an effort to support and enhance the *Closing the Gaps* program. Among the initiatives passed and funded are programs to enhance math education, a requirement that the recommended high school curriculum now be designated as the standard curriculum, and incentives to find and employ more certified teachers *(Closing the Gaps)*. Efforts to improve education in Texas have been a priority for recent governors, including Ann Richards and George W. Bush.

State officials also recognized that Hispanics have a lower rate of college attendance than whites or African Americans, and that the Hispanic population of Texas, which is now at 32%, is expected to continue to increase (Arnone). The master plan includes goals for increases in college attendance for all groups, but especially for minority students. As of now, Texas is not meeting its goals. For Hispanic students, only 15% of the goal has been met to date and for African American students, the figure is 28% (Arnone). The Texas Higher Education Coordinating Board reported in 2004 that Hispanic enrollment had increased by 54,565 students in the first three years of the initiative, an average increase of 18,188 Hispanic students annually. However, to meet the 2015 goal, the annual increase needed to average 23,520 students. (*Closing the Gaps*).

These circumstances make the affirmative action situation in Texas even more important. In response to the ruling in *Hopwood,* the state legislature enacted legislation requiring state universities to admit students who graduate in the top 10% of their high school class (Springer). In fall, 1997, the first year that state institutions were affected by *Hopwood* and prior to the implementation of the ten percent plan, the University of Texas had just 150 African American students in its freshman class of 6500 students, a decline of half from the year before (Pressley).

Studies show that before *Hopwood,* African American students made up 3.7% of enrollees at Texas A&M, but just 2.4% after the ruling. Numbers for Hispanics were also down from 12.6% before the ruling to 9.2%. For the University of Texas, African American enrollment dropped from 4% to 3.3% and Hispanic enrollment dropped from 15.8% to 13.7% (Axtman). According to UT Law School Professor Douglas Laycock, "Everybody wants a magic bullet that increases diversity without considering race. Well, there isn't any magic bullet" (Axtman).

The concept of automatic admission for students in the top 10% of their graduating class is certainly an interesting one, and the plan has attracted attention and scrutiny from around the nation. Admissions through this process account for about 70% of the freshman class at the University of Texas (University Business). Such plans enjoy the support of President Bush, while affirmative action does not. The U.S. Civil Rights Commission studied the Texas plan, along with similar plans in Florida and California, and reported in late 2002, "this analysis reveals that in each of the three states that have replaced [affirmative action plans] with percentage plans, minority students are faring the same or worse" (U.S. Civil Rights Commission).

The Court's Rulings

On June 23, 2003, the Supreme Court issued its long awaited rulings on affirmative action. By a 5-4 vote, the Court upheld the University of Michigan's Law School program that considers race as a factor in admission. In writing for the majority, Justice Sandra Day O'Connor said, The Constitution "does not prohibit the law school's narrowly tailored use of race in admissions decisions to further a compelling interest in obtaining the educational benefits that flow from a diverse student body." You will probably recall from your earlier reading that a *compelling* interest is an important legal standard, and you can see that in this ruling the Supreme Court continued to recognize diversity in higher education as a compelling interest (Springer). The five votes in favor of upholding the use of affirmative action in law school admissions came from Associate Justices O'Connor, John Paul Stevens, David Souter, Ruth Bader Ginsburg, and Stephen Breyer. Dissenting were Chief Justice Rehnquist and Associate Justices Antonin Scalia, Anthony Kennedy, and Clarence Thomas.

In a second ruling, by a vote of 6-3, the Supreme Court struck down as unconstitutional the undergraduate admissions policy at the University of Michigan. That policy had assigned a specific number of points or weight to minority students and students of low socio-economic background. Justice O'Connor was the key member of the Court, as she voted to uphold the law school admissions policy, but voted to overturn the undergraduate admissions policy.

In August 2003, the University of Michigan established a new undergraduate admissions policy that still considers race, but drops the point system. A university official noted, "We continue to believe in gathering a group of students that are very bright but different from one another" (CNN).

Conclusion

Is the national discussion about affirmative action over now that the Courts have ruled on the Michigan cases? Not likely. Affirmative action remains an important and controversial public policy issue about civil rights, so the national debate is likely to continue.

PRO & CON
Should Standardized Tests Be Eliminated
From the College Admission Process?

Taking the SAT is a stress-filled experience that has just become even more demanding with the addition of an essay in 2005. Our performance could determine where we will go to college and whether we can pursue the career we want. It is easy to see why we view those few hours as pivotal for our future.

Is it rational and logical for one test to be so important? Colleges and universities seem to think so because for several decades, most of them have relied on standardized test results to determine to a great degree just who will be admitted. There is debate about their value, however, and some believe that such tests should be eliminated from the college admission process.

YES, standardized tests for college admission should be eliminated.

The National Center for Fair & Open Testing opposes the use of the SAT and has adopted the goal of ending "the abuses, misuses, and flaws of student testing" (National Center). The State of Texas agrees that, at least for high-achieving students, the SAT or ACT is unnecessary. Scores of a certain level are no longer required for students who graduate in the top 10% of their high school class.

There are good reasons to stop using the SAT or ACT. The first reason is that standardized tests are poor indicators of student performance in college. At best, test scores provide an indicator of what a student's grades will be for the first year, but even that is not very reliable. After all, some students simply blossom in college, having found high school boring or irrelevant.

Second, standardized tests can measure only certain skills such as reading and writing. They make no attempt to measure many types of talent and ability, such as the ability to lead, to play music, to act, to paint, or to debate. All of those are important talents, but none is measured by the SAT or ACT. Standardized tests don't pretend to measure athletic talent and ability either, a fact recently recognized by the National Collegiate Athletic Association. The NCAA decided in the fall of 2002 to permit athletes with excellent high school records to bypass taking a standardized test to enter college. Prior to the change, student athletes were required to have a minimum score of 820 on the SAT to be eligible for admission (Lederman and Suggs).

A third good reason to stop using standardized tests is that they are culturally biased, a fact that has been common knowledge for a long time. According to The National Center for Fair & Open Testing, "The SAT has always favored students who can afford coaching over those who cannot, students from wealthy suburban schools over those from poor urban school systems, and men over women" (National Center). Additionally, many talented students for whom English is a second language may be disadvantaged by the test being so carefully timed (National Center). As we work to rid our society of the vestiges of discrimination and unfairness, surely the standardized test should be on the cut list.

Finally, there are many factors that contribute to a person's suitability for admission to college. After all, what every admissions officer is trying to do is assess the fit between the institution and the student, admitting students who will thrive in a particular setting. How can just a few factors provide sufficient guidance? It is time to consider other factors, including high school grades; types of courses taken; recommendations from teachers and counselors; community service; leadership potential and experience; special talents such as those in music, art, debate, and drama; and motivation. With so much to consider, why is it important to know the performance of a student on one test on one particular day?

NO, standardized tests for college admission should not be eliminated.

College admissions officers are faced with difficult decisions every day. Along with scores on standardized tests, they consider high school grades and class rank, participation in high school and community activities, letters of recommendation, and awards and honors the applicant has earned. Most officials would agree that basing their decision on just one factor would indeed be unfair, but admissions officers consider many factors in deciding whether or not to admit an applicant. Do standardized tests have a place in admissions policies for colleges and universities? Yes, there are several reasons to continue the use of the SAT and ACT.

First, colleges need some indicator that an applicant can perform at the college level, and the standardized test can provide that assurance. After all, these are tests of skill, measuring vocabulary, reading ability, analytical ability, and math skills, all of which are important to success in college. Why not, you say, just rely on that fabulous high school record? Because we all know that high schools vary considerably in their standards, so comparisons of students from different high schools are just not possible. Moreover, grade inflation is rampant these days, and almost everyone has a fine high school record. With so many excellent high school records, a test score can provide illumination of the student's preparation for college level work.

Second, standardized tests can actually save colleges money if the tests do nothing more than identify students who are not yet prepared to do college work. Millions of dollars are invested every year providing remedial courses that will not bring students one credit closer to a college degree. All these courses are meant to do is try to get students to the point where they are prepared to undertake college level work. Perhaps students who lack the academic foundation to read, write, and compute at the college level should be required to spend a year at a community college, and then reapply for university admission.

Third, there is evidence that standardized tests have been culturally biased in the past, but it is hard to continue to make that argument. Great efforts are being made to correct any and all biases in tests. If particular groups such as women, African Americans, Hispanics, or urban students show a group score lower than that of white, suburban male students, it should be possible to normalize the scores so that any bias is accounted for and excluded.

Finally, if we cannot trust standardized tests for college admission, we ought to be willing to get rid of such tests altogether, whatever their purpose. Why should we continue to test children at various grade levels if tests are faulty? Why should teachers have to take exams to show that they have the skills to teach? After all, any results would be unreliable and unfair. Why should prospective federal or state employees, accountants, attorneys, physicians, social workers, hairdressers, or anyone else have to take a test? The reason is that tests do have validity. They measure some skill or knowledge that has been deemed essential for whatever educational or professional endeavor we are pursuing. If you were hiring a new employee, would you prefer to hire the person who scored 95 on your entrance exam, or the one who scored 55? If you were a college admissions officer, would you prefer to admit the student who scored 1400 on the SAT or the one who scored 900?

Standardized tests may not be perfect measures, but they are reasonable and useful measures and, therefore, serve an important purpose.

The Concept of Equal Protection:
Two Important Cases

According to the Fourteenth Amendment, "No State shall deny to any person within its jurisdiction the equal protection of the laws." It is a controversial legal concept that has required many rulings from the Supreme Court. Here are two important cases that originated in Texas.

Sweatt v. *Painter,* 339 U.S. 629, 70 S.Ct. 848, 94 L.Ed 1114 (1950)

You probably already know that in the past, Texas had laws segregating state universities, including the University of Texas. When Herman Sweatt applied to attend law school at the University of Texas, he was turned down on the basis of his race. At that time, Sweatt sued because no law school in Texas admitted African American students. Because of the separate but equal doctrine, Texas officials responded to Sweatt's case by establishing the Texas College for Negroes. The quality of that new institution became an issue when Sweatt refused to register there and the matter went to the Supreme Court. In writing the Supreme Court's opinion in *Sweatt*, Chief Justice Vinson compared the highly ranked University of Texas Law School with the new law school that had been created for African American students: 1) While the University of Texas Law School had sixteen full-time and three part-time faculty members, the new school would have opened with just four part-time University of Texas professors whose offices would have remained at the University of Texas; 2) The University of Texas law library had more than 65,000 volumes while almost none of the 10,000 ordered for the new law school had arrived; 3) The University of Texas Law School was fully accredited, but the new school had no accreditation. There were other comparisons, too--all arriving at the same conclusion: the new law school for Blacks was in no way comparable to the University of Texas Law School, and the State was violating the Equal Protection Clause. The Supreme Court directed the University of Texas to end race discrimination and integrate its law school.

Phyler v. Doe, 457 U.S. 202, 102 S.Ct. 2382 (1982)

The case of *Phyler* v. *Doe* dealt with a Texas law that would have cut off state funds to school districts for illegal alien children attending those schools. The law also permitted local districts to charge the parents for the education of their children. Attorneys for the state had argued that denying education to the children of illegal immigrants might help the state cope with illegal immigration. They reasoned that people would think twice before coming illegally to the United States if they knew that their children would be denied an education. Another argument made by Texas was that it had an interest in conserving the state's resources, and one way to do that was to save the money that was otherwise spent on educating illegal aliens. The Supreme Court struck down the Texas law as unconstitutional, rejecting the state's arguments.

EXERCISE 6-1
Ending Segregation at the University of North Texas

In 2004, the University of North Texas celebrated the fiftieth anniversary of integration on our campus. A number of events marked this milestone in the University's history. Explore how UNT ended segregation and the important figures whose courage and actions made the change at UNT. You can find the information you need at the University of North Texas web page.

I.   Summarize the story of ending segregation at UNT, being sure to provide dates and names.

_____

_____

_____

_____

_____

_____

_____

II.   Compare and contrast the UNT story with that of another university which did not peacefully and quietly integrate.

_____

_____

_____

_____

_____

_____

_____

_____

Name		Seat	Score

EXERCISE 6-2
Congressional Black Caucus

The Congressional Black Caucus is an important force in the U.S. Congress. This exercise provides an opportunity to become familiar with the work of the CBC. Consult the CBC's website for information, making sure that to provide up-to-date information.

1.   What is the mission of the Congressional Black Caucus?

_____

_____

2.   Who chairs the CBC?

_____

3.   The web site for the CBC includes a discussion of several important issues. Select three issues to read about and summarize the key points of the CBC's views on each.

Issue #1:   _____

_____

_____

_____

Issue #2:   _____

_____

_____

_____

Issue #3:   _____

_____

_____

_____

Name		Seat	Score

EXERCISE 6-3
LULAC

As the fastest growing minority in the United States, Hispanics constitute an important political force. The League of United Latin American Citizens (LULAC) works on behalf of the rights of Hispanics. Consult LULAC's website for answers to these questions.

1.   LULAC was formed by three other organizations. What were those organizations?

      a.   _____

      b.   _____

      c.   _____

2.   When and where was LULAC established?

      _____

3.   LULAC has filed suit in many cases to promote the rights of Hispanics. What were three of those cases, including the legal issue in each?

      Case #1:   _____

      _____

      Case #2:   _____

      _____

      Case #3:   _____

      _____

4.   Many (but not all) of LULAC's initiatives have been through the courts. In the space below, identify three actions of the organization that have taken place outside of the courts.

      Action #1:   _____

      _____

      Action #2:   _____

      _____

      Action #3:   _____

      _____

5.   LULAC has a platform that details the organization's position on political issues of importance to Hispanics. For each of the issues below, identify in a complete statement the position LULAC has taken on the issue.

Issue #1:   Affirmative Action

_____

_____

_____

Issue #2   Racial Profiling

_____

_____

_____

Issue #3:   English as the Official Language

_____

_____

_____

Issue #4:   Bilingual Education

_____

_____

_____

Name		Seat	Score

EXERCISE 6-4
Civil Rights of the Disabled

Since the 1950s, many groups in our society have asserted their right to equal opportunity and treatment. The Americans With Disabilities Act (ADA) was enacted to protect the rights of the disabled, many of whom suffer unemployment and poverty. This exercise offers opportunities for you to become more knowledgeable about the ADA by answering questions about specific aspects of the law. Good sources of information about the ADA include the U.S. Department of Justice and the Equal Employment Opportunity Commission.

PART I: Basic Facts About the Americans With Disabilities Act

1. _____ In what year was the ADA signed into law?

2. _____ Which U.S. President signed the ADA into law?

3. Identify four aspects of employment that are covered by the ADA.

   a. _____   c. _____

   b. _____   d. _____

4. According to the ADA, who is a "qualified individual with a disability?"

   _____

   _____

   _____

5. An employer need not provide an accommodation if it would present what type of hardship for the company? In the space below, explain the type of hardship and provide an example of such a hardship.

   _____

   _____

   _____

6. What is the definition of a *reasonable accommodation* under the ADA?

   _____

   _____

   _____

PART II: Each of the following scenarios involves issues dealt with by the ADA. Based on your research, explain how the action involved is in accord with the ADA or in violation of it.

Scenario #1: A company hires an individual who uses a wheelchair. There is an employee lounge that employees use for breaks and lunch and that is sometimes used for company functions, such as staff meetings. Must the company modify the lounge so that it is accessible to the new employee?

_____

_____

Scenario #2: The interviewer suspects that a job applicant has a disability and requires that the applicant submit to a physical exam by the company's physician to ascertain the existence and extent of the disability before a hiring decision is made.

_____

_____

Scenario #3: At a particular company, all applicants are tested for illegal drug use. Upon being informed that his drug test came back positive, the applicant informs the interviewer that he cannot be rejected for the job on that basis, as his addiction is covered under the ADA.

_____

_____

Scenario #4: An employee qualifies under the ADA for accommodation. Identify and explain five types of accommodation that a business or educational institution might be required to make for the individual.

_____

_____

_____

_____

_____

Name		Seat	Score

EXERCISE 6-5
Women in the Work Force

To answer the questions below, go to the web site for the Women's Bureau in the Department of Labor (www.dol.gov/wb). Data can be found throughout the web site, including Resources & Information/Statistics and FAQ.

1. Each occupation listed below is one of the top 20 in which women are employed. Complete the table by listing the percentage of workers in each occupation who are women and the median weekly earnings of women in the field.

Occupation	Percentage of Persons in that Occupation Who are Women	Median Weekly Earnings of Women in that Occupation
Secretary		
Cashier		
Registered Nurse		
Elementary School Teacher		
Hairdresser, Cosmetologist		
Bookkeeper		
Secondary School Teacher		
Receptionist		
Waiter, Waitress		
Nursing Aides		

2. What percentage of the jobs in each of these categories is held by women?

    Dentists _____   Construction _____
    Police Officers _____   Pest Control _____
    Architects _____   Taxi Drivers _____
    Physicists _____   Air Traffic Controllers _____
    Firefighters _____   Truck Drivers _____

3. _____ About how many females over the age of sixteen live in the United States?

4. _____ How many women are part of the work force?

5. _____ Women make up about what percentage of the U.S. labor force?

6. The Women's Bureau names the seven occupations in which women have the highest median weekly earnings. Please list them in the space below:

    _____   _____

    _____   _____

    _____   _____

    _____

7. If a woman is pregnant, does she have any legal protection for her job? Explain.

_____

_____

_____

8. Clearly, there are occupations in which women make up a majority of workers. In many cases, those jobs are also low paying compared to others in which women do not dominate. Think about this issue and write below your assessment of why this situation exists. Is it because women tend to go into low paying jobs? Or is it because women are willing to accept lower pay than men, and employers are able to pay less because women dominate in these jobs?

_____

_____

_____

_____

9. Why is it that women tend to make lower salaries than men in U. S. society? Identify and explain three reasons, only one of which can be discrimination.

a. _____

_____

b. _____

_____

c. _____

_____

Name		Seat	Score

EXERCISE 6-6
Chapter Review

Select the best answer for each question below. Answers to all questions can be found in this chapter.

1. _____ Affirmative action is constitutional because the courts have found that it advances a/an

   _____.
   A. important national goal   C. compelling national objective
   B. law enacted by Congress.   D. significant purpose.

2. _____ In which part of the U.S. Constitution do we find the Equal Protection Clause?
   A. The Fifth Amendment   C. The Fourteenth Amendment
   B. The Tenth Amendment   D. The Twenty-second Amendment

3. _____ Affirmative action began with the issuance of an executive order by _____.
   A. President Kennedy   C. President Nixon
   B. President Johnson   D. President Ford

4. _____ Universities support affirmative action programs because they embrace the goal of _____.
   A. equal protection   C. fairness
   B. civic responsibility   D. diversity

5. _____ The case of *Regents of the University of California v. Bakke* dealt with
   A. a white applicant denied admission to medical school.
   B. a minority faculty member who was paid less than a white male hired at the same time.
   C. a law school admissions policy with a quota system for each racial and ethnic group.
   D. an undergraduate program that based admissions on a point system.

6. _____ The cases the Supreme Court agreed to rule on in 2003 began over affirmative action
   admissions policies at the University of _____.
   A. Southern California   C. Texas
   B. Maine   D. Michigan

7. _____ President Bush decided that his administration would side with
   A. the university and its affirmative action programs.
   B. the students who filed suit against the university's affirmative action programs.
   C. neither side, saying that his administration would be neutral on the issue.
   D. keeping affirmative action, but changing it slightly.

8. _____ The *Hopwood* case in Texas concerned
   A. white students denied admission to the UT Law School.
   B. minority students denied admission to Texas A&M.
   C. white students claiming reverse discrimination over policies at the University of Houston.
   D. minority students denied admission to medical school at the University of Texas.

9. _____ In response to the *Hopwood* ruling, the Texas attorney general decided
   A. to establish affirmative action in all Texas colleges and universities.
   B. to end affirmative action at the University of Texas.
   C. to end affirmative action in all Texas colleges and universities.
   D. to wait for a ruling from the U.S. Supreme Court on affirmative action.

10. _____ After *Hopwood,* the Texas legislature responded by passing a law to
   A. create an additional law school so that more Texans could study law.
   B. allow students who graduate in the top 10% of their high school class to have automatic admission to state universities.
   C. raise the test scores necessary to graduate from high school.
   D. create a state system of testing in order to raise educational standards.

11. _____ The initiative called *Closing the Gaps* recognizes that Texas
   A. must continue affirmative action, whatever the Supreme Court rules.
   B. needs to build more public colleges and universities.
   C. has neglected its public schools, which is now harming colleges.
   D. has a lower percentage of its population attending college than other states.

12. _____ A special problem the State of Texas recognized in *Closing the Gaps* was that
   A. too few Hispanic students are attending college.
   B. too many remedial courses are being offered at state institutions.
   C. too few professors have higher degrees in the field they are teaching.
   D. Texas urban areas often lack public colleges and universities.

13. _____ The term *reverse discrimination* refers to the claim that
   A. quotas actually harm everyone in society.
   B. the person least likely to deserve promotion often receives it.
   C. those who benefit from affirmative action suffer from its effects later.
   D. white males are harmed by affirmative action programs

14. _____ Florida banned affirmative action in higher education, replacing it with the One Florida Plan
   A. which guarantees college admission to the top 10% of graduating seniors.
   B. which guarantees college admission to students who score at least 1000 on the SAT.
   C. which guarantees a generous college loan program for good students.
   D. which lets teachers recommend the best students for college admission.

15. _____ Concerning the University of Michigan's undergraduate admissions policy that used a point system, the Supreme Court
   A. declared the policy constitutional, and the University has maintained it.
   B. declared the policy unacceptable, so the University has changed it.
   C. has not yet ruled.

Name		Seat	Score

CONGRESS: REPRESENTATION, GOVERNANCE, AND LEGITIMACY
Elizabeth A. Oldmixon and James Coleman Battista

The Founders designed the U.S. Congress to be a representative and a governing institution. Both are important functions, and Congress has secured its legitimacy over the years by performing both in a way that garners continued public support. As the representational and governing demands have changed in each new historical era, Congress has shown a remarkable ability to adapt and cope. The current era presents Congress with an array of governing challenges, and it is not yet clear how these will be met.

What Does Representation Mean?

Representation can mean a number of things. In a descriptive sense, it refers to a matching of demographic characteristics between legislators and the polity. For example, does the proportion of African Americans or women in the United States match the proportion of African Americans and women serving in Congress? Certainly African Americans and women have unique policy needs, so it is theoretically important that those populations be represented in their proper proportions in order to give voice to those needs. Some scholars question how representative Congress is if it is not descriptively representative.

Representation might also refer to the allocation of benefits and services from the government to different constituencies. Regardless of the collective demographic characteristics of the legislature, if elected officials can adequately provide services to constituents – such as service academy nominations or assistance dealing with the bureaucracy – and benefits to the district – such as federal pork projects – Congress is said to be representative. Some have even suggested that representation depends on the ability of elected officials to develop personalized relationships with their constituents. If they can do that, then they have earned their constituents' trust and have the freedom to behave in Washington as they see fit.

The most conventional way to think about representation is in terms of policy congruence. To what extent are the policy attitudes of constituents reflected in the attitudes and roll call voting behavior of the elected representatives? If we find congruence between the attitudes of constituents and behavior of representatives, the level of representation in Congress is evaluated positively. Of course, this kind of representation is difficult to achieve for a number of reasons. Some constituencies are very diverse, which makes it difficult for even well intentioned representatives to mirror the views of their districts. Also, on many issues, constituents do not have coherent policy positions.

Regardless of how you understand the concept of representation, the system of frequent Congressional elections (particularly for the U.S. House of Representatives) coupled with the minimal requirements for a) running for Congress and b) voting in Congressional elections should promote representation in Congress. Viewed in allocation terms, the level of representation in Congress is quite high. Legislators have structured the institution in ways that facilitate the allocation of benefits and services (Fiorina, 1989; Mayhew, 1974). For example, members of Congress have staffers that exclusively provide constituent service. In a descriptive and policy sense, Congress probably does not measure up quite as well, but at the very least, constituents are given the opportunity to select new representatives if they are dissatisfied in this area.

Governance and Legitimacy

"All legislative powers herein granted should be vested in a Congress of the United States, which shall consist of a Senate and House of Representatives" (U.S. Constitution, Article I).

It is not a coincidence that the legislative branch is laid out in Article I of the Constitution. As the above quote indicates, the Constitution places the responsibility of lawmaking – of governing – in the hands of Congress. Article I, section 8, goes on to elaborate a rather impressive list of legislative powers. The ability to govern, then, is another important standard by which we evaluate Congress.

It is through the proper exercise of these governing powers that Congress maintains its legitimacy. Legitimacy is the sense on the part of a polity that the current political system is legally and morally entitled to govern. Legitimacy does not imply that the governed have any great affection for government or even agree with what government does. It means that the people consent to be governed by a particular political system. Poll data below seem to make this point.

"How much of the time do you trust the government in Washington to do what is right?"	
Just about always	05%
Most of the time	29%
Some/none of the time	66%
"Whatever its faults, the United States still has the best system of government in the world."	
Agree	83%
Disagree	15%
Don't know	02%

Source: ABC World News Tonight "Listening to America" Poll, conducted by telephone from April 30-May 6, 1996, with a national sample of 1024 adults.

Few Americans trust government to do what is right "always" or "most of the time." Nonetheless, Americans express high levels of support for the government. Public support for Congress fluctuates. In a February, 2003 poll taken by the Gallup organization, only 50% of respondents expressed approval of "the way Congress is handling its job." Even so, Americans do tend to express high levels of support for the institution – even when they do not like what it does (Hibbing and Smith, 2001).

Throughout American history, the continued legitimacy of Congress has depended on its ability to skillfully govern. As Dodd (1993:419) writes, "Congress and its members must demonstrate a reasonable capacity to recognize fundamental problems of a historical era, deliberate over the proper solutions to these problems, and enact legislation that addresses them in a credible manner." For the most part, Congress has been adept at identifying the key issues of an era and addressing them legislatively.

When failures have occurred, they have been colossal. An inability to resolve the issue of slavery in the 19th century gave way to the Civil War. But, when industrialization created a battery of national problems, such as corporate corruption and child labor, Congress responded with a series of progressive-minded legislative solutions. The Great Depression demonstrated

the vulnerability of American workers to market forces beyond their control, and Congress and President Roosevelt responded with the creation of a bureaucratic service state designed to deliver services and support to displaced workers. World War II and the Cold War taught American policymakers the importance of international engagement. Congress responded by supporting the growth of the military-industrial complex and international military and economic commitments (Dodd, 1993). After September 11, 2001, it was members of Congress who first pushed for a reorganization of the federal government and the creation of the Department of Homeland Security to protect Americans on their own soil.

While there have been failures along the way, since the end of the Civil War Congress has demonstrated a reasonable capacity to deal with the salient issues that capture the national consciousness in a given era. In consistently demonstrating its capacity to govern, Congress has maintained a sense of legitimacy among Americans.

New Challenges in a New Era

Stateways cannot regulate folkways.
(William Graham Sumner)

Since September 11, 2001, our politics have largely been defined by the terrorist attacks of that day and our response to them. Congress and President Bush have both responded in ways that show innovation in the face of new challenges. However, other enduring issues mark the current era as well, and some scholars worry that Congress has yet to demonstrate an institutional capacity to handle them (Huntington, 1973).

Society underwent many changes in the 20th century. One important change has been the move from an industrial to a post-industrial economy. This means that we have a high-tech economy driven by technological innovation, service (as opposed to factory) based employment, and a highly educated workforce. Among the many consequences of this economic transformation that scholars have identified is that citizens will expect the government to deal with an emerging set of moral issues (Dodd, 2001; Lowi, 1998). Sumner's popular aphorism, which is quoted above, has often been parsed as, "You can't legislate morality." While that rings true to many, the U.S. Congress legislates morality every session. For example, in the 109th Congress, Congress placed itself squarely in the moral debates over Terri Schiavo and in the 108th Congress, legislators considered a constitutional amendment banning gay marriage. These issues present Congress with distinct governing challenges.

An individual's sense of morality gives him or her strong feelings about how people ought to live their lives and what kinds of social arrangements and relationships ought to be promoted and condoned (Wuthnow, 1987). Should women work outside the home? Should abortion be legal? Should contraception be readily available? Should we pray in public school? Should same-sex couples be allowed to marry? These are all moral questions.

Why will Congress have to deal with these issues? There are a number of answers. First, questions of morality are not local problems. Rather, they are national in scope, and they reflect who we are as a people and what values we share. If you believe same-sex couples should be allowed to marry, you probably believe that right should apply to gay and lesbian couples whether they live in Texas, or Arkansas, or Vermont, or the 47 other states. On the other hand, if you think homosexuality is immoral, you will probably find it unconscionable for some states to condone homosexuality in any way. Your preference will most likely be for national level condemnation. Second, in the 20th century, Congress and the courts redefined federalism such that the national government became more involved in policy areas traditionally reserved to the states. Finally, moral issues tend to be easy for people to understand and important to constituents.

It is important to understand that when Congress or any legislature regulates morality, this almost always involves the regulation of some private behavior. Whether one is pro-life or pro-choice, watches pornography or does not, supports physician-assisted suicide or not, we might all concede that government policies in these areas call into question—for better or worse—our individual autonomy, our freedom. In a liberal culture such as the one in the United States, scholars and political scientists alike have always placed a premium on the importance of individual freedom. When Congress legislates

morality, it may have the effect of limiting personal freedoms for the sole reason that their exercise offends a segment of the population (Smith, 2001). Congress may end up regulating an area of a person's life that many have argued should be off limits.

Moral issues challenge Congress for a number of reasons. First, "while much law codifies rights and wrong," moral issues engage values on which there is "no overwhelming consensus in a polity" (Mooney, 2001:4). As Mooney (2001) notes, there are many criminal activities that most people agree are wrong and deserving of state sponsored punishment—kidnapping, theft, and rape, to name a few. Prohibitions against these activities are all, to some extent, based on the value we place on individual integrity—integrity of one's person and one's possessions. No such consensus exists when we are dealing with fertility control, prayer in school, or physician-assisted suicide. When Congress deals with these issues, many people will have a fundamental conflict with values embodied in it by the policies it enacts. Therefore, it will be difficult to deal with these issues in any way that provides closure or resolution.

Second, many people are hypocrites with regard to these issues (Meier, 2001). Public pronouncements and private behavior are often at odds. People decry as immoral what they themselves do or have done in the past. For example, public opinion data indicate that Americans overwhelmingly disapprove of pornography and see it as a threat to society. Yet the demand for pornography is high. In 1995, adult video rentals comprised 28% of all rentals in certain regions of the country. It was a half-billion dollar industry (Smith, 1999). This means that members of Congress and other politicians do not get an accurate feel for what the public wants, and that makes it difficult for them to be honest with their constituents about what they really believe. No member of Congress wants to be seen as "standing up for sin," being the champion of sex, drugs, and the destruction of the American family (Smith, 2001).

Third, moral issues do not easily give way to compromise because the political lines of battle are drawn between good and evil, morality and sin. The following are quotes from the *Congressional Record* taken from debates on two very contentious moral issues – abortion and gay marriage. They illustrate the contentious nature of these issues in Congress.

". . .those of us who are pro-life see this as a matter of principle [pro-life], not just as an issue that can be compromised. We really do see this issue of abortion as a matter of life and death, as a matter of taking away a life that God has allowed to be created as the object of His love" (Rep. Poshard, Nov. 1, 1995, *Congressional Record*, page H11683).

"The very foundations of our society are in danger of being burned. The flames of hedonism, the flames of narcissism, the flames of self-centered morality are licking at the very foundations of our society: the family unit. The courts in Hawaii have rendered a decision loud and clear. They have told the lower court: You shall recognize same-sex marriages" (Rep. Barr, July 12, 1996, *Congressional Record*, page H7482).

The stakes for legislators and their constituents are very high. The passions among pro-choice and pro-gay rights legislators run equally high. If you feel that compromise offends God's will, how do you do it? If you feel that women will only be equal citizens if they have the right to choose an abortion, how do you compromise on that? Congress, however, is an institution with rules and norms designed to facilitate compromise. Of the 7,000 to 10,000 bills that are introduced in Congress each year, only a few hundred are actually enacted into law. The legislative process is long and complicated, and the vast majority of bills die in committee. For a bill to run the gamut of the legislative process and achieve passage, different groups of legislators – Republicans and Democrats, liberals and conservatives, senators and representatives – almost always have to strike a compromise between what they want and what will pass. No one gets everything, but everyone gets something. An inability to compromise can lead to gridlock on important issues.

The fate of the Partial Birth Abortion Ban Act of 1995 provides an excellent example of this. This legislation would have prohibited the procedure of partially vaginally delivering a fetus,

killing the fetus, and completing the delivery, unless the life of the mother is in danger. Critics of the legislation wanted to amend it to allow a health of the mother exception. The Republican leaders kept the amendment off the floor, preventing representatives from having the opportunity to vote on it. The amendment was widely supported in the House and almost certainly would have been agreed to. With that amendment President Clinton indicated that he would have signed the bill. A real compromise was available to legislators. They could have enacted legislation that practically eliminated the partial birth procedure, but it did not happen. Opponents of the amendment feared that a health of the mother exception would provide an enormous loophole for people trying to get around the legislation. Since the amendment was never considered and never agreed to, President Clinton eventually vetoed the legislation.

Conclusion

"[T]here's a bias that being ethical means standing alone....We think we're the only righteous person here in Sodom on the Potomac....A case needs to be made for cooperative work on a committee and in a party setting....And I think there's an ethical burden of proof on the person who will not cooperate in doing what needs to be done to bring policies to fruition" ~ Rep. David Price (D-NC), Interview with author of essay, July 19, 2000.

For more than 200 years, the U.S. Congress has served as the nation's representative and governing institution. It has shown a remarkable ability to adapt to each new historical era, improving its performance in both areas. Congressional action has been key to expanding voting rights and, by extension, representation to groups such as women and people of color. Time and again it has shown its ability to identify and address issues of common concern. In demonstrating its ability to govern with each new historical era, Congress has maintained a sense of legitimacy in the eyes of most Americans.

In the post-industrial era, Congress has confronted many new challenges. Certain moral issues have emerged as highly salient to many Americans, and the push is for national solutions to the problems reflected in these issues. Congress has confronted other moral conflicts in the past. It has demonstrated an ability to overcome the polarization these kinds of issues produce. However, it is not yet clear how Congress will adapt to the issues of the current era. Congress has legislated on these issues repeatedly, but never in a way that fully overcomes the lack of moral consensus, and never in any way that provides resolution to either side of the moral debate. Acceptable compromise has yet to be reached. The above quote from a Democratic Representative captures the frustration many legislators feel with this situation. The result is that legislators continue to submit legislation on issues such as abortion and gay rights, and lobbyists and constituents continue to push Congress to legislate in these areas.

It would be a gross overstatement to suggest that the legitimacy of the institution is hanging on its ability to learn to legislate morality. National security and the economy are on the forefront of the national consciousness, and it is on these issues that Congressional legitimacy hangs. However, the moral issues are not going away, and they will continue to provide the subtext for much of American politics. The real danger is that polarization on moral issues will spill over into other areas. Arguably, the current problem confirming judicial nominations stems from this conflict. If Pat Buchanan is right and there is a culture war in the country, it's being fought in Congress. If this produces more partisanship and more gridlock, if this inhibits the ability of Congress to govern, the institution will – at least for a time – be weakened. However, students of Congress should be impressed and heartened by Congress's capacity to learn, and then adjust to new challenges. If a time comes when resolution of the current moral conflicts becomes critical for the nation and the legitimacy of the institution, there is every reason to believe that Congress will rise to the challenge.

PRO & CON
Should Texas Adopt Term Limits For Its Legislature?

YES: Term limits increase representativeness.

Term limits would help Texas keep from moving further down the road towards a professional, career legislature. We need to make sure that the Texas legislature represents all Texans and that Texans from all walks of life are able to serve in the legislature for a term or two before returning to real life in their chosen profession. If the legislature remains unlimited, we should expect it to eventually be filled with the same sorts of full-time career politicians who overwhelmed the legislatures of other large states like New York and California. These career politicians will drive out the homemakers, small business owners, educators, and other ordinary citizens who should be able to serve the public good in the legislature.

Term limits bring in new blood and new ideas.

Term limits mean that nobody and no point of view can become an entrenched power in the legislature. As people in Texas develop new ideas, new points of view, and new ways of thinking, term limits will help those new views get represented in the legislature. This is because it will not be possible for long-term members to make sure that people with ideas they are frightened of or disagree with are held powerless in the legislature, because there won't be any long-term members. New legislators will arrive in sufficient numbers to force the legislature to at least listen to their new ideas instead of assigning them to pointless committees. Term limits also mean that legislators will come from a real job in the real world, so their new ideas will reflect real-world experience with how the laws they pass actually affect Texans.

Term limits decrease conflicts of interest.

One of the problems with career politicians is they understand that, with every election, their whole career is on the line. This leads to their willingness to sell out their constituents in favor of special interest dollars to fund their next election. Term limits eliminate this problem. On the one hand, term limits will help keep those career politicians out of the legislature in the first place. On the other hand, term limits mean that legislators will not have to, year after year, mingle and schmooze with representatives of special interest groups, and they will find it harder to maintain the close contacts that are necessary for the career politician / interest-group complex to last. Term limits mean that legislators will respond to ordinary Texans, not to special interests.

Term limits foster a more efficient citizen legislature.

Term limits will even reshape how the legislature operates. In a professional, full-time, career-politician legislature like Congress or in the states of New York and California, it can take two, four, eight, or even more years to get an important bill passed. These delays are one tactic that career politicians can use to frustrate new people with new ideas — it tells them that if they want to effect the change that their constituents sent them to bring about, they have to stay in the legislature for a long time instead of working in their chosen profession. In a term-limited legislature, everyone would know that they only have a few years to get their bill through and passed. This means that the legislative process will become more efficient because legislators will be forced to act on legislation. It means that you won't see an unfair, undemocratic emphasis on seniority (how long a member has been in the legislature) because there will be a hard limit on how long a member can serve. This will give new people with new ideas a better, fairer opportunity to get their bills passed promptly.

NO: **Term limits are undemocratic -- "Stop me before I vote again!"**

The greatest problem with term limits is that they deprive voters of their democratic right to elect whomever they wish to elect. The essence of democracy is that any qualified citizen can stand up and ask for the right and responsibility to serve in any elective office. Term limits flips this on its head – it says that maybe you were qualified to serve last year, but now that you've gathered more skill and experience you're no longer qualified to serve *even if the people in your district want you to serve.* Term limits, by their very definition, can only kick out members who have been elected several times – members who have been approved by their constituents time and again. A limit on terms would force Texans to stop sending their best, chosen candidates to the legislature and allow them to send only their second-best or third-best candidates. It might be that you don't like whom the district next to yours is sending to the legislature, but is that really any of your business?

Term limits decrease experience.

Term limits would create a legislature dominated by inexperienced new members. These new members might have work experience as lawyers or teachers or homemakers, but they will not have experience legislating. They will not have experience writing laws, leaving them more likely to write bad laws with loopholes that can be easily exploited by special interests. They will not have experience with which laws work and which don't, leaving them more likely to unnecessarily repeat in Texas what an experienced legislator would know didn't work when it was tried in Wisconsin and Florida.

Term limits increase conflicts of interest

Term limits serve to increase conflicts of interest in the legislature. Proponents of term limits argue that term limits will create a legislature with bankers, doctors, homemakers, and educators serving a term or two and then returning to their jobs. This sounds good at first, but whose interests will these people be serving? If a bank executive leaves his or her job to take a job as a legislator for a salary of only $7200 per year, should we believe that he or she really intends to serve the common good of Texas? Or should we believe that he intends to benefit the banking industry at the expense of consumers, so that when he goes back to the banking job he can move up the corporate ladder? Will physicians serving for two or four years in the legislature see their "real" constituents as their district or their profession? Further, term limits create opportunities for corruption. Term limits usually let a legislator serve for eight to twelve years – enough time for a third or a half of a career. This means that there will be legislators who know that they're going to be forced from office at the end of their current term with few real-world skills. Surely some will be tempted to sell out Texas in favor of some special-interest group if that group can promise them a cushy job when they leave the state legislature.

Congressional Reapportionment and Redistricting

In 1789, the first House of Representatives had sixty-five members. House membership kept growing from 1789 until 1910, reflecting the population growth in the nation. After each national census, taken every ten years, states gained house seats, and, of course, new states were being added to the Union, too. Following the census in 1910, however, legislation capped the membership of the House at 435.

Now, after each census, the 435 seats in the House are redistributed, based on population growth and population shifts. For membership to remain at 435, a state must lose a House seat for another to gain one. Here in Texas, the population has continued to grow, so Texas has gained seats in the House after the 1980, 1990, and 2000 censuses. Following the 2000 census, Texas gained two House seats, putting the total at 32 representatives in the Texas delegation to the U.S. House.

The population of the United States is not only growing. It is shifting as well, especially toward the so-called *Sunbelt* states such as California, Arizona, Texas, and Florida, and away from the so-called *Rustbelt* states such as Michigan, Ohio, and Wisconsin. Typically, the colder climate states lose seats to the warmer states after each census.

The process of redistributing representation in the House is called *reapportionment*. Because each member of the House is elected to serve a specific geographic area, a congressional district, the district lines must also be redrawn--a process called *redistricting*. Redistricting U.S. House districts as well as state legislative districts is the responsibility of each respective state legislature and has always been a contentious process. State legislators have continually sought ways to manipulate redistricting to achieve certain goals. When state legislatures are unable to complete the redistricting process, courts have to step in to finalize district lines.

Political gerrymandering takes place when district boundaries are drawn to the advantage or disadvantage of a particular political party. It has been common practice throughout our history. We know, for example, that Patrick Henry led an effort to gerrymander the county containing James Madison's home to prevent Madison's election to Congress because of Henry's alleged opposition to the Bill of Rights.

In modern times, in a Republican-controlled state legislature, Congressional districts are drawn in such a way to promote the election of Republicans to Congress as well as to the state legislature. In other states where Democrats control the state legislature, they gerrymander districts to elect the most Democrats to Congress (and to the state legislature as well). The Supreme Court thus far has refused to declare political gerrymandering unconstitutional.

Redistricting remains a highly contentious and political process. Nowhere is this more obvious than in Texas! After the 2002 elections, the Republican party had majorities in both branches of the Texas legislature as well as being in the Governor's mansion, and the new majorities set out to redraw district lines in their favor. This caused such an uproar among Democrats that some left the state for Oklahoma and, later, New Mexico in order to prevent the Senate from having a quorum to pass the redistricting bill, though a bill did eventually pass. This happened because both Republicans and Democrats understood that districting is important and fundamental to gaining and keeping control of political office. Because the stakes were seen as so high, both sides were willing to employ tactics that they might not have been willing to use for more normal, day-to-day issues.

EXERCISE 7-3
Understanding the Differences Between the House and Senate

The framers of the Constitution designed a bicameral national legislature consisting of a House and a Senate. This exercise should help you understand some of the differences between the two chambers. Use your textbook and the Constitution to fill in the blanks and answer the questions below.

		House	Senate
1.	What is the term of office?	_____	_____
2.	How many legislators serve in each chamber?	_____	_____
3.	When the Constitution was ratified, how were legislators selected?	_____	_____
4.	What is the title of the presiding officer?	_____	_____
5.	What is the age requirement?	_____	_____
6.	What is the citizenship requirement?	_____	_____
7.	How many Representatives/Senators come from each state?	_____	_____

8. The Constitution specifies a distinct role for both the House and the Senate in the impeachment of public officials. Explain the roles played by each chamber.

_____

_____

_____

9. The Founders' design intended for the House and Senate to represent different constituencies. The Senate was to represent the states, and the House was to represent the people. Why?

_____

_____

_____

10. List three differences between the House and Senate that facilitate the representation of states versus the people.

   a. _____

   _____

   b. _____

   _____

   c. _____

   _____

11. Explain one important difference in the way that the House and Senate consider legislation.

   _____

   _____

   _____

12. _____ *True or False.* The House of Representatives has the authority to ratify treaties.

13. _____ *True or False.* All revenue bills must originate in the House.

14. _____ *True or False.* In the appointment of public officials, both the Senate and House are required to provide advice and consent to the president.

15. _____ *True or False.* With the ratification of Amendment XVII to the Constitution in 1913, the people of each state could directly elect senators.

Name		Seat	Score

EXERCISE 7-4
Congress in the Constitution

1. Who judges disputes about House elections?

    _____

2. What limitation is imposed on funding the Army?

    _____

3. Does Congress have the power to coin or to print money?

    _____

4. In the original Constitution, did the states have power to coin or print money?

    _____

5. May journals of the House and Senate be edited for secrecy?

    _____

6. When may Congress suspend the writ of habeas corpus?

    _____

7. How many votes are needed in the House or Senate to expel a member?

    _____

8. In which chamber must bills about taxation be introduced?

    _____

9. How big a vote do you need to override a presidential veto?

    _____

10. What amendment gave Congress the power to create an income tax?

    _____

11.   What restrictions are there on convicting someone for treason?

_____

_____

_____

12.   When are members of Congress immune from arrest, and what are the exceptions to this?

_____

_____

_____

13.   What rules of the House and Senate are contained directly in the Constitution?

_____

_____

_____

14.   List two powers specifically forbidden to Congress.

_____

_____

_____

Name	Seat	Score

THE CHIEF EXECUTIVE
Patrick T. Brandt

The Development of Presidential Powers

Article I.1 *All legislative Powers herein granted shall be vested in a Congress of the United States, which shall consist of a Senate and a House of Representatives.*

Article II.1 *The executive Power shall be vested in a President of the United States of America.*

With these two simple sentences, the Founding Fathers created the two most powerful institutions in the new modern American democracy. Note the basic differences, however, in these two sentences: "All" legislative power is granted to Congress, but "The" executive power is granted to the president. Why the difference? Is it of any consequence for the powers of the presidency? What are the powers of the president? How have these powers changed?

Presidential powers have been transformed significantly since the writing of the Constitution. The personalities of presidents, the events of history, and the changes in American society have altered the role of the president and his powers. This essay examines the origins of presidential powers and outlines some of these major changes over time.

After a long series of debates at the Constitutional Convention in Philadelphia in the summer of 1787, the participants settled on creating a single executive. But, they did not enumerate a list of powers for the new president (in contrast to what they did for Congress in Article I, Sections 8 and 9). Thus, the president was given roles as Commander in Chief, Chief Diplomat, Chief Legislator, Chief Bureaucrat, and Chief Magistrate. But he, unlike Congress, was not given a list of formal powers in each of these areas.

What the Founding Fathers did create was a Presidency that tried to redress the problems of executive power that were familiar to them. They created a weak executive on paper. What were the factors that led them to create an executive that on paper was so weak?

First, the recent experiences of the thirteen original colonies with the King of England, George III, left the Founders skeptical of creating a strong executive. Instead, they lodged the major powers of government policymaking in Congress.

This extended to war-making powers, which had typically been the prerogatives of monarchs. The King of England had possessed the sole authority in waging war and dealing with foreign powers. In the American experiment, the Founders split this power between the president and Congress. The president can negotiate treaties, but no treaty can go into effect without the consent of the Senate. In addition, the president is commander in chief of the armed forces, but Congress retains the power to declare war and the "power of the purse," which is the right to make decisions on how and for what purpose federal tax revenues will be spent (Fisher, 2000).

Second, after the Revolutionary War, the original colonies wrote new state constitutions that included various efforts to define executive power. These were mixed successes, ranging from the strong governorships in New York to the weak and nearly non-existent executive power of Virginia. The key problem the Founders faced in writing a new constitution to replace the Articles of Confederation was a need to balance executive powers with those of the legislature. They sought to do this by separating powers across the branches of government (executive, legislative, and judicial) and requiring a system of checks and balances that provided a means for each branch to check the worst excesses of the other(s).

Finally, the Founding Fathers had to create an executive to address the fact that *there was no executive or president under the Articles of Confederation* that had formed the national government after the Revolutionary War. This failure to create an executive under the Articles of Confederation had seriously hampered the Congress, forcing it to create numerous legislative committees to oversee the executive functions of government or to appoint executive administrators for the various departments of government. This system was ineffectual for two reasons: first, it took time away from the Congress's efforts to engage in legislative functions, and second, it required them to hire and create positions for executive administrators. Without some day-to-day method of overseeing them and granting them executive power, these administrators were basically useless and many of them refused to remain in office.

The Founders' Solution to Executive Power

What was the Founders' experiment to create executive power in the "New" Constitution? The Founders separated the executive, legislative, and judicial functions. They created a system where the president shared powers with the other branches of government, in effect, creating competition among the branches. This system---the separation of powers and checks and balances---was the answer. The Constitution created an executive whose powers were limited only by the vague wording of Article II, and the limits of power that a president might successfully claim. As James Madison noted in *Federalist 51*,

> In order to lay a due foundation for that separate and distinct exercise of the different powers of government, which to a certain extent is admitted on all hands to be essential to the preservation of liberty, it is evident that each department should have a will of its own.... But the great security against a gradual concentration of the several powers in the same department consists in giving to those who administer each department the necessary constitutional means and personal motives to resist encroachments of the others. The provision for defense must in this, as in all other cases, be made commensurate to the danger of attack. *Ambition must be made to counteract ambition* (Madison et al., 1787, emphasis added).

To Madison and the Founders, the solution to creating an executive branch was to be sure that the other branches were sufficiently strong to resist any efforts by the executive to gain more power. This meant creating a strong Congress and making it the center of the national government.

For the presidency, this meant insulating the president from popular opinion by having him indirectly elected via the Electoral College. Further, the president was forced to exercise his power to enforce laws subject to those written and reviewed by Congress. Finally, Congress had a say in foreign policy and the use of military force. The president was allowed to negotiate treaties and appoint ambassadors, but required to submit each to the Senate for approval. And, the president could not exercise the sovereign's or King's right to declare and wage war; only Congress could declare war.

The presidents of the 19th century were, for the most part, significantly weaker than the presidents we know today. Their veto power over congressional legislation was rarely used, and when it was exercised, the public and Congress expected it to be on legislation that was considered unconstitutional. As presidential scholar Robert Spitzer notes, President John Tyler's two vetoes of national bank bills in 1841 led to such outrage that he was likened to Judas Iscariot, and he was nearly impeached before the end of his term (Spitzer 1993). In addition, the early years of the Republic were known as a period of strong Congresses to which the president was expected to be subservient.

Changes in the Nature of Executive Power

Debates about the nature and interpretation of presidential power began almost immediately after the founding of the country. George Washington's Secretary of Treasury Alexander Hamilton and Secretary of State Thomas Jefferson disputed the role of the national government in the economy and the president's authority to issue the Neutrality Proclamation of 1793. Washington issued the Neutrality Proclamation to keep the U.S. out of the war between France and England. Hamilton and Jefferson then began a very public debate about the nature of the president's constitutional power to issue the Neutrality Proclamation. This debate, waged in newspapers (like the Federalist-Anti-Federalist debates surrounding the Constitution) saw Hamilton defending the President's proclamation under the pseudonym Pacificus. Jefferson, not wishing to oppose Washington, enlisted James Madison (then a member of the House of Representatives) to write letters under the name Helevidius opposing the president's power to issue proclamations. The ensuing Pacificus-Helevidius Letters were an important debate over the nature of executive power and whether the president had the power to issue proclamations. Madison, writing as

Helevidius, argued that declarations of neutrality were a function of the president's power to make treaties and therefore required legislative action by the Senate (Nelson, 1999).

Changes in the nature of presidential power were a major component of pre-Civil War politics. The election of Andrew Jackson in 1828 (after he had lost the election in the House of Representatives in 1824) marked a major change in the presidency. Jackson advocated a populist presidency and argued that the president should be chosen by and responsive to the American people (not the Congress). Toward that end, Jackson vigorously exercised and expanded the presidential veto power. Jackson issued more vetoes in his presidency (1829-1837) than had all his predecessors. He also expanded the use of the presidential veto as a policymaking tool. Presidents since Washington had exercised the veto only for minor legislation that they argued was unconstitutional. Jackson, however, exercised the veto over legislation that he disagreed with on policy grounds. This, coupled with Jackson's use of the pocket veto, reshaped the power of the president to negate congressional actions.

Starting with the Civil War and the presidency of Abraham Lincoln, there was a significant change in the interpretation of the limits of presidential power. Lincoln argued in 1864 in a letter to Albert Hodges, the publisher of a Kentucky newspaper, that

> I did understand, however, that my oath to preserve the Constitution to the best of my ability imposed upon me the duty of preserving, by every indispensable means, that government—that nation, of which that Constitution was the organic law. Was it possible to lose the nation and yet preserve the Constitution? By general law, life and limb must be protected, yet often a limb must be amputated to save a life; but a life is never wisely given to save a limb. I felt that measures otherwise unconstitutional might become lawful by becoming indispensable to the preservation of the Constitution through the preservation of the nation. (Letter to Albert Hodges, reprinted in Pfiffner and Davidson, 2003)

This view of presidential powers, one that allows the president to contravene the Constitution ("amputate a limb") to preserve the nation ("save a life") was a sweeping interpretation of presidential powers. Lincoln subscribed to this *prerogative theory* of presidential power as a means to deal with the Civil War. He reasoned that in times of national emergency, presidents might actually have to violate the Constitution to preserve the nation.

Lincoln's theory of presidential power was short-lived and unprecedented in American politics. Later Congresses worked to assert congressional powers and reign in the excesses of the post-Civil War presidents (Fisher, 2000; Spitzer, 1988).

Theodore Roosevelt, who became president in 1901 following the death of William McKinley, advocated an expansion of presidential powers that he called the *stewardship presidency*. Roosevelt articulated his beliefs about presidential power in his 1913 autobiography:

> My view was that every executive office, and above all every executive officer in high position, was a steward of the people bound actively and affirmatively to do all he could for the people, and not to content himself with the negative merit of keeping his talents undamaged in a napkin. I declined to adopt the view that what was imperatively necessary for the nation could not be done by the President unless he could find some specific authorization to do it. My belief was that it was not only his right but his duty to do anything that the needs of the nation demanded unless such action was forbidden by the Constitution or by the laws. Under this interpretation of executive power I did and caused to be done many things not previously done by the President and the heads of the departments. I did not usurp power, but I did greatly broaden the use of executive power. In other words, I acted for the public welfare; I acted for the common well-being of all our people, whenever and in whatever manner was necessary, unless prevented by direct constitutional or legislative prohibition....(Roosevelt 1913).

Roosevelt's new conception of the presidency led to dramatic policy changes and expansions of the president's sphere of influence in the American constitutional system. Roosevelt exercised significant policy leadership and waged public campaigns to win passage of progressive legislation. His actions were a first in American politics, using what he called the "bully pulpit" of the presidency to win public support for his policy initiatives and to deal with resistance in Congress. Roosevelt's expansion of presidential powers led to significant policy changes that have affected American life and politics ever since: the strengthening of economic regulation of railroads in the Hepburn Act of 1906 served as a message to monopolies not to overcharge and engage in price discrimination. To win support for the Act, he campaigned vigorously across the country after the bill failed to pass Congress. When the Act was reconsidered in 1906, it passed overwhelmingly, due to Roosevelt's significant pressure (Milkis and Nelson, 2003).

Roosevelt's strengthening of the president's relationship with the public and his stewardship view of the presidency led to other policy changes. He was able to encourage progressive Republicans in the House and Senate to buck their conservative leadership and approve new policies that had popular support. Roosevelt also pushed the first major presidential legislative program, the "Square Deal" in 1904, cementing the president as a legislative leader and the chief legislator. Roosevelt also set aside large tracts of national forests for conservation and professionalized the federal civil service.

Some of Roosevelt's greatest policy achievements came in expanding presidential powers in foreign policy. Roosevelt expanded the U.S. role in the world to protect the territories gained in the Spanish-American War. This active foreign policy led to the creation of the Panama Canal Zone (after backing a revolution for Panamanian independence from Columbia), an expansion of the Monroe Doctrine to protect U.S. interests in Latin America, and a commitment to back the Japanese with possible offensive actions in the Russo-Japanese War of 1905. These actions presaged the expansion of U.S. foreign policy that would come into full bloom after World War II (Milkis and Nelson, 2003).

Roosevelt's successor and former Vice President, William Howard Taft (1909-1913), had a much more restricted view of presidential power. Like his 19th century predecessors, he believed in a limited presidency. Taft argued that the president was to carry out the laws as written by Congress and

...that the President can exercise no power which cannot be fairly and reasonably traced to some specific grant of power or justly implied and included within such express grant as proper and necessary to its exercise. Such specific grant must be either in the Federal Constitution or in an act of Congress passed in pursuance thereof (Taft, 1916).

Taft's limited, or *strict constructionist theory* of the presidency, was a final effort to return to the constrained presidency of the 19th century. Taft, however, was no match for the precedent set by the media savvy master of the bully pulpit, Theodore Roosevelt.

Woodrow Wilson, the only president to hold a doctorate, defeated Theodore Roosevelt and William Howard Taft in the 1912 presidential election. Wilson drew strongly from the Roosevelt presidency and argued that the president was not only a steward, but also a political leader of his party both within and outside Congress. Wilson thus ushered in the idea of the *public* or *rhetorical presidency*. To Wilson, the presidency had grown with the nation. He wrote,

In the view of the makers of the Constitution the President was to be the legal executive; perhaps the leader of the nation; certainly not the leader of the party, at any rate while in office. But by the operation of forces inherent in the very nature of government he has become all three, and by inevitable consequence the most heavily burdened officer in the world. No other man's day is so full as his, so full of responsibilities, which tax mind and conscience alike and demand an inexhaustible vitality.... And in proportion as the President ventures to use his opportunity to lead opinion and act as spokesman of the people in affairs the people stand ready to overwhelm him by running to him with every question, great and small.... But we can safely predict that as the multitude of the President's duties increases, as it must with the growth and widening activities of the nation itself, the incumbents of the great office will more and more come to feel that they are administering it in its truest purpose and with greatest effect by regarding themselves as less and less executive officers and more and more directors of affairs and leaders of the nation, — men of counsel and of the sort of action that make for enlightenment (Wilson 1908).

What a contrast to his predecessor Taft! In three successive presidents we see a radical transformation of the office of the presidency and its powers. While Taft harkened back to the earlier presidencies of the 19th century, Wilson and Roosevelt forged ahead. Wilson advocated a view that the president was the public face of the nation, the leader of his party. In these roles the president could hardly be anything but the center of attention in national politics. He was to guide his party, both on national issues and in Congress. The president was to be the leader of the country, a shaper of public opinion, and the leader of his party.

Executive Power in Modern Times

This transformation of presidential power and the public roles of the President reached its zenith in 1932 with the election of Franklin D. Roosevelt (FDR) to the White House. A distant cousin of Republican President Theodore Roosevelt, Franklin Roosevelt was elected as a Democrat as the Great Depression worsened. Roosevelt faced a national crisis upon taking his oath of office in 1933: failing banks, millions out of work, depressed agricultural production, and failing credit markets. All of these combined to create the most severe economic crisis in American history.

Franklin Roosevelt greatly expanded the public perception and powers of the presidency in order to combat the Great Depression and to wage the Second World War. Upon taking office, FDR issued the Bank Holiday Proclamation, closing all the banks in the nation for three days to avert a banking crisis. He expanded the role of the federal government in creating social insurance

with the signing of the Social Security Act of 1935. Roosevelt expanded the size and scope of the national government through the New Deal.

These transformations were hard fought: Congress's efforts to empower Roosevelt led to Supreme Court decisions (*Humphrey's Executor v. U.S.* and *Schechter Poultry v. U.S.*). that would have reduced the legal power of the president to regulate the economy and pursue the economic revitalization of the New Deal. FDR's effort to pack the Supreme Court with justices sympathetic to the New Deal, while a failure in the end, sent the Court a message that reverberated throughout the remainder of the 20th century: presidential power and congressional actions would not be limited by 19th century views of the limited role of the presidency and federal power.

Roosevelt's strong leadership on economic reforms and the prosecution of World War II set a new high-water mark for presidential powers. Later presidents would draw upon the new presidential mold created by FDR to understand the use and exercise of the office. In 1934, the Supreme Court's decision in *U.S. v. Curtiss-Wright* authorized the president to exercise significant powers in foreign policymaking. This decision led to a revised understanding of Roosevelt's exercise of presidential powers in foreign and military affairs – including such actions as Lend-Lease aid to Britain in World War II and Roosevelt's diplomatic negotiations with Churchill and Stalin about the composition of post-World War II Europe at Yalta in 1945. Congress was never consulted about what the nature of the division of Europe should look like, but rather was presented with a *fait accompli* after the war.

Roosevelt's expansion of the role of Commander in Chief in World War II set the stage for leadership during the Cold War. Subsequent presidents have felt little need to require congressional authorization or declaration for war for military engagement before the fact (Fisher, 2000). The expanded U.S. role in world politics since 1945 and the Cold War have been at the root of increased involvement. With this involvement has come the need for rapid responses.

President Truman continued the great expansion of presidential powers by engaging the U.S. in the Korean War without a formal declaration of war. Truman was reined in by the Supreme Court decision in *Youngstown Sheet and Tube v. Sawyer* when he attempted to seize steel mills to prevent a steel worker strike. Truman claimed that the mills were essential to the Korean War effort. He was, however, rebuffed by the Supreme Court, which viewed the action as not permitted by congressional statute even in times of national emergency.

Conclusion

The presidential powers of the Constitution are a source of continued conflict in the American political system. Because the Founders did not create a specific grant of presidential powers (like they did for Congress) and because of their inherent distrust of executive power, the result has been a separation of executive and legislative power that is open to interpretation and change. The Founder's solution was to create an executive separate from Congress and to require that under the separation of powers the president and Congress work together to achieve major policies. In the intervening 215 years since the adoption of the Constitution, this solution has seen revision as national events, presidents, and even Congress itself have sought to modify presidential powers. As a result, debates over the powers of the presidency today owe a great deal to the actions and personalities of past presidents.

PRO & CON
Should the President Be Allowed to Send Troops Abroad Without Consulting Congress?

YES! Presidents in their role as Commander in Chief should be able to do anything necessary to protect Americans and the American national interest at home and abroad. The president is the only national actor who can respond quickly to changing national and international events. The president has access to specialized intelligence and military information that may require quick action. He should be able to take this action for the well-being of the American public. The president must be able to exercise his emergency powers by sending troops any place in the world to defend our country.

Presidents have a long history of using military force to defend U.S. interests. U.S. troops have been committed to overseas operations over 200 times in American history, although Congress has declared war only five times. The president, however, can responsibly use military force to defend U.S. interests as he did during the Cold War or, more recently, in operations in the former Yugoslavia, Afghanistan, and Iraq.

The president's role as chief diplomat also means that he must act to meet American obligations in international treaties such as the North Atlantic Treaty Organization, the United Nations Charter, and mutual defense treaties. Many of these treaties allow for the United States to come to the defense of other nations and to protect U.S. interests oversees, such as free trade, democracy, and the safety of American citizens. Since the Senate has approved these treaties, the president is within his powers and authority granted by Congress to send troops without consulting Congress. This is because Congress knew there was a potential that U.S. troops could be sent under one of these treaties.

Congress cannot foresee every possible contingency for military action. Further, Congressional deliberations do not allow for quick action, and even if Congress were to act quickly, it would be unable to tailor legislation to adequately direct military action in defense of the United States. Finally, even if the president is able to commit troops oversees, the War Powers Resolution of 1974 and Congress's appropriations powers allow Congress to retain a role in commitments of troops overseas.

NO! The Constitution requires that only Congress has the power to declare war. The president commands the troops, but it is Congress that has the authority to raise and support an army and navy under the Constitution. This authority also includes determination of how the army and navy are to be engaged in conflict and when to use militias to prevent insurrection and invasions.

Congress in the past has authorized major uses of military force overseas. The War of 1812, the Mexican-American War, the Spanish-American War, and World Wars I and II were declared wars. In addition, minor uses of force by the United States have been authorized by congressional statute even if war was not declared. The authorization of military operations by statute occurred in the Quasi-War with France, the Barbary Pirate Wars, the Indian Wars, and the Whiskey Rebellion. Thus, Congress has been and should continue to be involved in troop commitments overseas.

Recent efforts by presidents to engage military forces overseas in the Korean War, the Vietnam War, the NATO interventions in Bosnia and Serbia in the 1990s, the Gulf War, and our involvement in Iraq and Afghanistan were all undertaken without formal declarations of war. Significant numbers of troops were committed in these operations and past commitments of U.S. troops are not a strong basis for recent actions. Past actions were justified by U.S. interests, while these more recent military actions were done on the basis of the U.N. Charter, the North Atlantic Treaty Organization (NATO), and mutual defense pacts with other countries. These two treaties both allow the Congress to exercise its constitutional role to declare war and regulate the use of U.S. troops abroad. Thus, even if the Senate approves a treaty that allows for the United States to defend its interests overseas, Congress still retains the right to authorize the use of troops in any particular conflict.

Congress should reassert its warmaking power and require the president to seek approval from Congress. This would be consistent with the 1974 War Powers Resolution that required the president to seek approval for any troop commitments of more than 60 days.

THE TWENTY-SECOND AMENDMENT
GLORIA C. COX

No person shall be elected to the office of the President more than twice, and no person who has held the office of President, or acted as President, for more than two years of a term to which some other person was elected President shall be elected to the Office of the President more than once.... ~ Twenty-Second Amendment, Constitution of the United States.

Only one person has been elected to the American presidency more than twice: Franklin Roosevelt. He won in 1932, 1936, 1940, and 1944, although he did not complete his fourth term. Each of his campaigns took place against the backdrop of important events. During his first two campaigns, Americans were suffering from the effects of the Great Depression, and, by 1940, World War II was already underway in Europe. Many Americans relied heavily on Roosevelt's leadership, as judged by public reaction when he died in office in 1945.

After his presidency, the Republicans in Congress wanted to make sure that no one could again dominate the presidency as Roosevelt had, so they spearheaded a drive for a constitutional amendment limiting any person to two terms (or ten years total, if a vice president ascends to the presidency to complete the term of a president who had died or resigned). The Twenty-Second Amendment was added to the Constitution in 1951.

It is difficult to find good people to run for president. For whatever reason, we perceive many candidates to be flawed, and, in fact, it is common for voters to view a presidential election as a choice between two unappealing, undesirable candidates. The lack of presidential material, or at least the lack of competent and appealing individuals who are willing to run for office, makes it all the more necessary to keep open the option of continuing with the person who is in office. For example, in 1988 many Americans questioned why they should have to choose between George H.W. Bush and Michael Dukakis when the very popular Ronald Reagan would have been available had it not been for the Twenty-Second Amendment. In 2000, many people would have preferred another chance to elect Bill Clinton rather than voting for Al Gore or George W. Bush. Interestingly, Mr. Clinton has recently voiced his support of repealing the amendment, as did Mr. Reagan.

Yet, do we really want to get rid of the Twenty-second Amendment? The presidency is one of the most demanding jobs in the world, and it takes a tremendous toll on the person. Eight years is long enough for any one human being to be president, given the strains and stresses the job holds. Although some Republicans called for repeal of the Amendment so that Ronald Reagan could run for a third term, we have seen the tragic illness Mr. Reagan suffered, and we recognize that it would have been inappropriate to put him back in office for a third term.

We also know that our nation benefits from the new ideas and fresh approaches that a change in leadership brings. Even a president popular enough to be elected again and again runs out of new ideas after a time. Problems may remain unsolved until a new leader comes along with innovative ideas and new approaches to the situation. Different people also bring different priorities to the presidency, making it possible to focus on one set of problems now and another during the presidency of another leader. Remember President Johnson, who could not seem to extricate the nation from the quagmire of the Vietnam War?

So what do you think? Is the Twenty-Second Amendment a good thing for the nation, or just an obstacle to the leadership we want?

EXERCISE 8-3
The Arguments of the Founding Fathers
Concerning Powers of the President

Alexander Hamilton, James Madison and John Jay wrote a series of essays that we now know as the *Federalist Papers*. Two of these papers, Numbers 69 and 70, written by Hamilton, are arguments for the presidency and limits on presidential power. You can read copies of the two papers at the Library of Congress site: http://memory.loc.gov/const/fed/fedpapers.html. After reading them, answer the following questions:

1. To what two other kinds of executives does Hamilton compare the President?

   a. _____

   b. _____

2. According to Hamilton in Federalist Number 69, a _____ cannot be removed from office by impeachment and trial.

3. The President's veto is considered to be _____ unlike the absolute veto of the King of England.

4. What are four differences between the Presidency and the King or colonial governors according to Federalist Number 69?

   a. _____

   b. _____

   c. _____

   d. _____

5. In Federalist Number 70, Hamilton argues that "Energy in the executive is a leading character in the definition of good government." What are the four components of executive "energy" in Hamilton's argument?

   a. _____

   b. _____

   c. _____

   d. _____

Name		Seat	Score

EXERCISE 8-4
The Twenty-Fifth Amendment & Presidential Disability

Please consult the Twenty-Fifth Amendment for answers to the questions below.

Scenario #1:   The president suffers an illness and dies. What does the Constitution provide?

_____

_____

Scenario #2:   The Vice President is involved in a scandal and resigns his post. Is there a way to select a new vice president?

_____

_____

Scenario #3:   The president has to undergo major surgery, and wishes to transfer his powers to the vice president temporarily. How does he do that, and how does he reclaim his powers later?

_____

_____

Scenario #4:   The president has lapsed into a coma from which doctors think he will never awake. What happens to the presidency in such a circumstance?

_____

_____

Scenario #5:   In the opinion of the vice president and members of the cabinet, the president is suffering from a mental illness. The president does not agree that he is ill. What procedure exists to make a determination about who will serve as president?

_____

_____

Scenario #6:   In some parts of the Amendment, the vice president becomes the president. In others, he becomes the acting president. What is the difference?

_____

_____

Name		Seat	Score

PROBLEMS OF CONTROL AND CAPTURE
James Coleman Battista

Bureaucratic Discretion, Control, and Capture

We often think of bureaucracies and agencies as being basically passive – if you want a driver's license or passport, you fill out some forms which are looked over by the people behind the counter to make sure you are eligible for the license (or other benefit), you pay a fee, then you receive whatever you have requested. The only real decision seems to be whether you filled out the forms correctly.

The truth is considerably more complex. Bureaucratic agencies actually have vast discretion about how to implement or to enforce legislative or executive policies. If your family gets in trouble for building in a wetland, you will not be fined because you violated a federal statute. What you violated is a regulation or rule created by a bureaucracy – in this case, the U.S. Army Corps of Engineers, an agency that defines what a wetland is and what people are allowed to do in wetlands.

Does this happen beyond wetlands? Do other agencies make definitions and decisions that affect who gets punished or rewarded, and for what? Yes! It is common for Congress (or state legislatures) to write laws that establish only vague guidelines for what policies should look like. In these cases, it is up to the responsible bureaucratic agency to take that abstract policy and turn it into specific rules and regulations that people can be punished for disobeying. For example, Congress sets vague environmental laws for soil contamination, but it is the Environmental Protection Agency (EPA) that decides exactly what levels of exactly what pollutants are permissible. While Congress decided that workplaces must be kept safe for their employees, it is OSHA, the Occupational Safety and Health Administration that decides exactly how high guardrails must be and what the fine will be for having a guardrail that is too low.

Why do public officials carry out the legislative function in this manner? One reason is specialization. Congress may be good at writing laws, but its members are not highly skilled specialists in any policy area, nor is the President. So, Congress concentrates on taking input from constituents, interest groups, and businesses, and then formulating broad outlines of policy to respond to public demands. For example, Congress might decide that because of popular or group pressure we need to substantially reduce smog in our cities. Members of Congress do not really know how to do this, because Congress isn't full of meteorologists, chemists, and atmospheric scientists–but the EPA is. Members of Congress have experience understanding public opinion and converting the needs and wishes of many different people into a coherent statement of public policy. Congress and the President, then, can rely on the technical expertise of the EPA to transform general policy and vague statements about smog control into a set of specific rules that industry can follow.

Or can they? How can Congress and the President know that the Corps of Engineers, or the Environmental Protection Agency, or OSHA is making rules that they would approve? After all, the agency is doing the implementation in part because the political branches do not have the necessary expertise. Would they even know if the agency wrote a rule that they did not like? The agency might have an incentive to try to issue a rule or regulation that it sees as appropriate, but that will anger or irritate enough people to cause some members of Congress, state legislators, or other elected officials to lose their job at the next election. How can Congress (or the President) make sure that an agency does what they want it to do instead of what the agency wants?

This is a common problem in human interaction, known as the principal-agent problem. Such problems happen when one person (the principal) hires another person (the agent) to perform some task. If there is *asymmetric information*, the agent is operating under a set of facts and assumptions that are not the same as those of the principal. For example, the agent knows how hard he or she is working, but it's difficult for the principal to find out how hard the agent is working. This is similar to many jobs you have probably held, where *you* might have known that you could have worked harder and gotten more done, but your employer, your principal, would find it difficult to discover that you were pacing yourself, slacking off, or otherwise doing less work than you could have. In the real world, principals use three main tools to keep their agents in line: monitoring, incentive structures, and finding the right agent.

Monitoring is when the principal observes the agent to make sure that he or she is doing a good job. The problem with monitoring is that it is expensive in terms of the principal's time.

Incentive structures are when the principal gives the agent a share of the prize from the activity – salespersons working on commission have an incentive structure. The problem with incentive structures is finding the right set of incentives.

Finding the right agent is when you try hard to find an agent who wants the same things that you do – then there is no difference between what you want done and what the agent wants to do. For example, if you want an agency that will vigilantly pursue environmental concerns, you would want to hire people with pro-environmental beliefs who may have worked for Greenpeace or the Nature Conservancy. The problem here is ensuring that a prospective agent really does share your values and is not pretending just to get the job.

Overall, Congress and other legislatures, as well as the President and other executives, face two problems with bureaucratic discretion. The first is that of *control*: making sure that agencies promulgate (or create) rules that they view as appropriate. The second problem is that of *capture*, where an agency stops regulating in the public interest and begins regulating for the benefit of the industry it is supposed to be regulating.

Problems of Control

Methods of Control 1: Threats of Punishment
One primary method of control is the use of incentives. As it happens, Congress and the President do not really have many positive incentives to offer agencies, so they have to rely on negative incentives or the threat of punishment. The political branches, especially Congress, can promise an agency that it will be punished if it misbehaves.

How do you punish an agency? One way might be to take away some of the amenities of the people who work there. You might require them to keep their thermostats at less comfortable temperatures, or put their offices in undesirable parts of town with little parking, or other sanctions. While these are minor, the big gun that

Congress and the President have is control of agency budgets. If the agency does not follow political mandates, it might have its budget cut or even eliminated.

Is this likely? Is this a credible threat? If an agency actually called their bluff and set a rule that they did not like, would they actually want to cut their budget? The answer seems to be probably not. What happens if you cut the budget of some agency? Obviously, the agency gets hurt. But in addition to the agency, the people served by that agency are hurt as well. Agencies may even try to deal with a budget cut by making the public suffer so that constituents will contact their representatives.

An agency might sometimes promulgate rules that are so far from what Congress and the President want that they actually do cut their budgets, but this is a "lose-lose" situation. The agency loses because it made a mistake in thinking that its actions would be tolerated. At the same time, Congress and the President made a mistake in not communicating clearly enough what could be tolerated. What does punishment as a strategy to keep agency rule making in line tell us? Everyone has a strong incentive to avoid it, and agencies do not want to push the political branches too far. Congress and the President want agencies to have clear ideas of how much room they have to set their own rules and regulations.

Methods of Control 2: Appointments
A second method of control is to try to pick the right agent. The President appoints people of his choosing to run bureaucratic agencies, and the Senate has the power to confirm or deny those appointments. In this way, they try to hire people who guide their agencies according to what Congress and the President want, although the President is clearly the more important actor in this strategy. The key word is, however, *try*. It turns out that appointing people you like to head an agency is a largely ineffective method of control because agency heads do not actually have vast amounts of power over what the agency does. More accurately, if you appoint the right person, you might be able to keep the agency from passing rules and regulations that you do not like, but appointments do not help you make that same agency pass rules that you do like. The agency head can forbid something effectively, but if he or she tries to make something happen (if he or she

tries to make the agency issue a rule that it does not want to issue), bureaucrats have an amazing ability to delay and stall by simply insisting that all of the bureaucratic niceties be followed exactly before they do anything. It acts as a veto and as a negative control over implementing legislation.

Methods of Control 3: Hearings

A third strategy of control, belonging primarily to legislatures, is an example of monitoring. Congress can use its ability to subpoena bureaucrats and the politically appointed heads of agencies to inquire about exactly what an agency is doing. Agency representatives can be brought before the agency's authorizing committee or before a special or "select" committee and asked tough questions about what they are doing and why.

If you are a bureaucrat, how much should you worry about hearings being held about your agency? Perhaps not much, because monitoring is expensive in terms of the principal's time. Congress can hold all of the hearings it wants, but these take time and effort. Time is one of the most precious things to a Member of Congress. Time spent interrogating an agency spokesman is time not spent putting together a vote trade to benefit your district, or shaking hands with Boy Scouts from your district. It is rarely the best way to spend your time. Even when Congress does hold hearings, the ability to actually find out that the agency has been misbehaving is limited because their best source of information is the agency itself (which is not likely to be forthcoming about its own misbehavior).

Methods of Control 4: Procedures

This rounds out our discussion of how the three main solutions to principal-agent problems take concrete form in the interactions between Congress, the President, and agencies with rule-making discretion. There is another unique form of control over an agent. Congress and the President use *procedures* to their advantage. In particular, the Administrative Procedures Act of 1946 forces agencies to follow very specific, complex, and lengthy methods of decision-making before they actually issue a rule or regulation.

The exact method of decision-making varies somewhat from agency to agency and is beyond

the scope of this discussion in any case. However, some common features are:

- The agency must announce, well ahead of time, its intent to issue a new rule or change an existing rule.
- The agency must invite comment from all interested parties.
- The agency must hold hearings about the proposed rule, in which pressure groups can provide witnesses.
- When the rule is issued, the agency must explicitly state how the evidence it received in hearings (and from other sources) supports the rule.

Why does this matter? Look at this from the perspective of whether Congress and the President want to punish an agency. Control procedures like these do two things. First, they give pressure groups the ability and incentive to monitor the agency, so that Congress does not have to. Second, this monitoring allows Congress to step in and warn an agency *before* it does something so undesirable that it needs to have its budget cut as a punishment.

Political scientists refer to pressure-group monitoring of agency rule-making as "fire alarm" oversight as opposed to the more traditional "police patrol" oversight (McCubbins, Noll, and Weingast, 1987) When Congress or the President goes out and actively investigates, when they look for problems with agency rule-making, they are like a police patrol that is walking a beat. This may not be the best way for them to spend their time. Look at the steps involved in making a new rule: the agency must seek out relevant pressure groups and ask for their opinion about a proposed rule, so groups have the first look at the rule. Later, at the hearing stage, they have the right to bring witnesses, ask questions, and see how the agency seems to be leaning. This gives the pressure group a fire alarm to ring. They know that the Department of Veterans Affairs is about to do something that veterans will not like, or that the Department of Agriculture is going to do something that farmers view as harmful to their interests. This gives the pressure group a powerful incentive to complain to Congress (or the President) that the agency that is supposed to be helping them is about to harm them. Allowing the pressure groups a role in agency rule making gives them an alarm, and their own interests (or the interests of those they represent) give them every incentive to pull that alarm to avoid being harmed.

This works to the advantage of Congress (and the President, to a limited extent) in three ways. First, fire alarm oversight gives Congress all of the benefits of monitoring its agency (agents), but pushes the cost of monitoring onto the pressure groups. It is the pressure groups that must pay people to show up at the hearings to listen and contribute, not Congress. It is the pressure groups, not Congress, who find themselves poring over the *Federal Register* for announcements of upcoming new rules or rules changes that will affect them.

Second, even when a pressure group does not complain to Congress, the agency is still forced to respond to and deal with the same pressures that will eventually be applied to Congress by the pressure groups. This gives the agency a better estimate of what sorts of rules Congress will let it get away with, and an opportunity to withdraw the proposed rule before it does any harm.

Third, fire alarm oversight is embedded in a lengthy, drawn-out process. This means that pressure groups have plenty of time to complain before the rule takes effect, and before the agency does anything irrevocable. This means that after a pressure group complains, Congress has time to quietly and discreetly warn the agency that the rule it is thinking of will not sit well.

Controlling Bureaucratic Discretion in Texas

Does any of this change in Texas government? The core problem persists – governors and legislators in Texas face principal-agent problems with bureaucratic agencies. The main difference between the federal principal-agent problem and the one in Texas is that state governors and legislators have a much tougher time controlling their bureaucratic agents.

This points back to the Texas Constitution, which sets up a weak legislature and weak governorship. The nearly inevitable result is that bureaucratic agencies become more powerful (as do the numerous independent commissions that Texas uses to administer policies).

Monitoring is more difficult in Texas than in the federal government, especially for the legislature. This is largely because the Texas

legislature is not full-time. It meets for regular sessions of 140 days beginning in January of odd-numbered years. This means that the entire process of legislation, which might take a year or more in Congress, is compressed into a few months. With legislators busy writing bills, doing committee work, and trying to build a coalition to get bills passed, there is little time left for overseeing the bureaucratic rule-making process.

Selecting the right agent by appointment to head an agency is often impossible in Texas. Like many states, Texas has a plural executive. We elect many members of our state executive branch. Many positions that would be appointed in the federal government are filled by election in Texas. The practical upshot of this is that instead of working for the governor, many agency heads work directly for the people of Texas – or at least for the people who care enough about what their agency does to vote on the basis of their performance.

Punishment is never a desirable strategy to use in controlling bureaucratic rule making, because punishing the agency also punishes the governor or legislature by harming constituents. The Texas legislature and governor face more problems with punishment than their federal counterparts do. Before you can punish, you have to observe misbehavior, and this is more difficult to monitor in Texas. Further, the Texas Constitution limits the extent to which the legislature or governor can punish an agency. Like most state constitutions, the Texas Constitution is much longer and more specific than the federal Constitution. Some of this length and specificity is spent creating taxes and earmarking funds for certain uses by specific agencies. This means that some agencies are somewhat immune from threats of budget cuts because their funding is provided directly by the constitution instead of being under the control of the legislature.

Problems of Capture

A second main problem arising from bureaucratic discretion is that of *bureaucratic capture*. This idea comes largely from the economist George Stigler and his book *The Theory of Economic Regulation* (for which, among other accomplishments, he received the Nobel Prize for economics in 1982). The basic idea is that businesses and industries might want to be regulated.

Why would a firm or an industry want to be regulated? One answer is that regulations can sometimes limit the supply of your good and so increase its price. Many industries, such as law, accountancy, and cosmetology and hairdressing, are commonly regulated through licensing. This is ostensibly to protect the public, but it also serves to keep people from entering that industry (and driving wages down by doing so). Another reason is that regulation can sometimes help firms form cartels, or at least achieve much of what a cartel would accomplish.

The classic example of this is the Interstate Commerce Commission (ICC) and its regulation of the railroads. Because a single farmer had little market power, but a large industrial company had tremendous power, it was often the case (before the ICC was established) that a small farmer might pay more to ship his grain 50 miles to market than a large industrial firm paid to ship its goods across the country. This was because railroads competed with each other for the large contracts offered by large industrial firms. As might be expected, a cry for regulation went up, and the ICC was formed. By necessity, the ICC was created with input from the railroads and with ex-railroad employees. The ICC promptly began regulating, abolishing secret rebates to large shippers, making it illegal to offer the discounts that led to perverse-seeming rates, and so on. But what effect did this have? Did small farmers see any great reduction in their rates? No. What happened was that the regulations helped the railroads collectively exploit the large industrial firms---the discounts that they had been offering to compete with each other were now illegal! Nobody's price went down substantially, and the price that large industrial firms had to pay increased. (Congress eliminated the ICC in 1995, and its functions were distributed to other agencies, including the National Surface Transportation Board.)

Does this mean that capture is inevitable? No. Firms and industries sometimes fight hard against regulations that will actually cost them money. However, the point remains that it is worthwhile to look at an economic regulation with a skeptical eye---who is this regulation really going to help? Is it actually going to force firms to charge a lower, ostensibly fairer price, or is merely going to stop them from offering discounts to some people and thereby increase their profits?

PRO & CON
Should Agencies Be Run More Like Businesses?

YES: Agencies should be run more like businesses. If we were to give local agencies more freedom to hire and fire, instead of tying their hands with restrictive seniority rules and "civil-service" protections, we could encourage higher efficiency and increase levels of customer service. If we allowed agencies to determine what rules and procedures would serve them and their local community best, the needs of the local community would be better served, and a lot of red tape could be eliminated.

Efficiency

As it is now, agencies cannot easily fire bad workers. Civil service and seniority rules, while enacted with the good intention of eliminating political hiring and firing, have served only to protect the incompetent. We should give managers the freedom to fire people whose performance *they feel* is incompetent, not what a rulebook from Washington defines as incompetent. This will allow managers to sweep the deadwood from their agencies and run a more efficient shop, saving taxpayers money and doing more with the money they do spend.

Customer Service

Likewise, running agencies like businesses will improve customer service. When you are treated badly at the end of a line in one government agency or another, you know that no matter how rudely that employee treats you, his or her job is safe. Allowing a local manager to fire a rude employee will give the employees a strong incentive to treat their customers well. Likewise, managers who run a rude local agency would find themselves terminated from the job by a higher-level manager.

Local Needs

Agencies, like businesses, should be allowed to respond to their local environments. Currently, rules are set up in Washington to apply to New York and Maine and Kansas in exactly the same way. If a farmer is applying for aid, local agencies are in the best position to determine appropriate standards for who gets aid and who does not, because they know local conditions and needs.

Red Tape

Giving agencies the power to set their own rules and criteria would also help to eliminate insane levels of red tape. For example, if you are a young foreigner who wants to marry an American, forms require you to promise that you have never committed genocide, and that you were not a member of the Nazi party between 1933 and 1945 (even if you were born after that time). Then, once you have successfully entered the United States, you are required to promise the same things, again, and if you later wish to become a U.S. citizen, you have to make the same promise yet another time. The idea that someone who had actually committed genocide would check off that little box defies belief. If we were to allow local agencies to set their own rules, some of them would have the good sense not to use such silly rules, and those agencies would end up being the most efficient ones. Thus, their good habits would spread across the country, and we could rid ourselves of red tape.

NO: We should not allow agencies to run themselves like businesses, because they are not businesses. While the idea of greater efficiency is always appealing, it is doubtful whether running agencies along business lines would greatly improve efficiency. At the same time, running agencies like businesses could have calamitous results for the fairness and neutrality of our government.

Efficiency

It is possible that allowing managers more freedom to hire and fire would increase efficiency, and certainly some employees are slow, inefficient, or incompetent. But would allowing managers to fire whomever they please really help? There is no profit incentive to motivate them to lower costs, so there is nothing to prevent a manager from firing good workers and replacing them with his or her friends or relatives. The true efficiencies of businesses come from competition, not their ability to hire and fire. And we cannot have all agencies be competitive – if the driver's license agency were run competitively, surely the one that would make the most money would be the one with the most lax standards. While allowing hire-and-fire freedom *might* increase efficiency, it might also reduce efficiency if managers fire workers they personally dislike, or who belong to the wrong political party.

Customer Service

The same logic applies to customer service. Customer service is often poor because the offices are under-staffed and every worker has an excessive caseload, not because they merely delight in being rude. If we want to improve customer service, the answer is to fund the agencies at higher levels so that there are more front-line workers at the counters, or to provide workers with bonuses based on their customer service scores. If we do not improve working conditions, all we achieve is local agencies firing people as they "burn out" under their workload.

Local Needs

Allowing agencies to respond to local needs is also tempting. Government agencies, however, are not businesses. The Constitution guarantees equal treatment by the government, not localized and special treatment depending on where you live and what the people around you want. This means that if a farmer in Nebraska is eligible for aid, a farmer who is just the same except that he lives in Kansas should also be eligible, even if that person doesn't fit with what the local agency thinks is best. Additionally, we might worry that some local agencies might set up their "local needs" in such a way as to harm Black or Latino or other minority citizens, or in such a way as to benefit one political party.

Red Tape

Finally, this plan would not merely eliminate useless red tape. Government regulations often seem silly, but many of them are there for excellent reasons. Thick rulebooks and standard operating procedures exist so that someone on the ground, with relatively little training, can have access to the collective wisdom of the experts in their area. While there is no guarantee that the rules and procedures will be set up just right, not having them will also cause as much harm as good. It is not at all certain that people in a local agency will know which rules are actually useless or silly and which are important safeguards, and we ought not let them decide.

Texas Government Agencies

The Railroad Commission of Texas

In Texas, higher education, public safety and corrections, and public welfare account for four of every five state employees. It would be inaccurate, however, to assert that those are the only important agencies in the state bureaucracy. In fact, another Texas agency is routinely referred to as one of the most powerful agencies of state government to be found anywhere. The agency with those extraordinary powers is the Railroad Commission of Texas. The Railroad Commission of Texas was established in 1891 to regulate fees charged by railroads. However, its most important duties now are actually regulating oil and gas production in Texas, and its decisions have a direct effect on how much you (and people in other states) pay at the gas pump. The Commission claims that it is "the oldest regulatory agency in the state." It regulates commercial transportation and mineral extraction within Texas. The agency is headed by three commissioners who gain office by running in partisan elections.

The Texas Higher Education Coordinating Board

In 1965, the Texas legislature created the Texas Higher Education Coordinating Board (THECB) to oversee and coordinate developments in higher education. With 35 public universities and more than a million college students in the Texas (according to the agency web site), coordination is a necessity. Whenever a public university in Texas wants to take a certain action such as establishing a new doctoral degree program, it must first win approval of the THECB. Likewise, the requirement that there be a common core of general education requirements in all Texas public institutions by 1999 had to win the approval of the THECB before it could be implemented. In an earlier chapter of this workbook, you read about the Texas plan for higher education, *Closing the Gaps,* which is under the direction of the Texas Higher Education Coordinating Board.

Tremendous Variety

You may want to visit the web page for Texas government (at *www.state.tx.us*) and take a look at the listing of state agencies. You will find many agencies including the Alcoholic Beverage Commission, the Board of Barber Examiners, the Funeral Service Commission, the Real Estate Commission, the Commission on Human Rights, the Commission on Law Enforcement Officer Standards and Education, the Interagency Council on Sex Offender Treatment, the Department of Transportation, and the Workforce Commission. Many agencies deal with or regulate a narrow part of life, or a particular industry. In many of these agencies, the leaders are directly elected by the people and the governor and legislature have little control over them. Even when the governor can appoint the leaders, the agency is often still relatively free to go its own way. In the absence of a strong legislature and strong governor, Texas government has grown into a network of small agencies, each with strong powers in its own limited area.

EXERCISE 9-3
The Agencies Strike Back!

Bureaucratic agencies are not just passive actors that accept what happens to them. They have their own preferences and wants, and they have the ability to harm people who are trying to hurt them by cutting their agency budgets. The general principle is that if you have to make cuts, you should make them in a way that maximizes the pain to the general public. That way, people might complain to Congress to get your funding back. With that in mind, what would you cut, and what would you be sure not to cut, if you were the head of the following agencies and had your budget cut 20% to punish you? If you're not familiar with an agency, use your favorite search engine to find out more about it. Be clever, and be cruel!

Denton ISD

_____

_____

_____

The National Park Service

_____

_____

_____

The USDA

_____

_____

_____

Texas DOT

_____

_____

_____

Nuclear Regulatory Commission

_____

_____

_____

Name	Seat	Score

EXERCISE 9-4
Spot the Bureaucracy

Bureaucracies aren't found only in government, and not every governmental agency is a bureaucracy. Technically, an organization is a bureaucracy if it meets two criteria. First, it must have a definite hierarchy or chain of command. There is a real organization chart with everyone on it, and you know to whom you can give binding orders as well as who you have to take orders from. Second, the organization must have a definite set of procedures. This is harder to spot, but if there is a giant manual that tells you what to do, odds are it has a definite set of procedures. The idea is that you should be able to consult the standard operating procedure, or the manual, to deal with any situation that comes up. With that in mind, are the following organizations bureaucracies? Indicate whether or not they meet the two criteria, and if they don't, say why not. If you don't know much about an organization, look for further information on the Internet.

Organization	Hierarchy?	Procedures?
The U.S. House of Representatives		
The U.S. Marine Corps		
The Roman Catholic Church		
A fraternity or sorority		
Your PSCI 1040 class		
The UN Security Council		
Your electric company		

Name		Seat	Score

EXERCISE 9-5
Finding Information on the Net: Bureaucratic Agencies

Use the Internet to find answers to the following questions. You should use a good search strategy and your favorite search engine. Some good places to start are www.info.gov and www.firstgov.gov for federal information and www.state.tx.us for Texas information.

1. What is DARPA?

    _____

    _____

    _____

2. What federal department houses the Census Bureau?

    _____

    _____

    _____

3. List two subsidiary agencies of the Texas Department on Aging.

    _____

    _____

    _____

4. What is the title of the official who heads the U.S. Department of Justice?

    _____

    _____

    _____

5. Name two agencies within the U.S. Department of Justice.

    _____

    _____

    _____

6. What Texas agency issues marriage licenses?

    _____

    _____

    _____

7. What official heads that agency?

_____

_____

_____

8. How is the Nuclear Regulatory Commission headed?

_____

_____

_____

9. What official is the immediate superior of the Surgeon General?

_____

_____

_____

10. What federal agency (not department) owns the nuclear testing grounds of the Nevada Test Site, and to what department does it belong?

_____

_____

_____

11. What federal and Texas agencies regulate alcoholic beverages?

_____

_____

_____

12. To what branch of government does the Government Accountability Office report?

_____

_____

_____

Name		Seat	Score

THE COURTS
Kimi Lynn King

The role of the courts encompasses virtually every facet of American society. As Alexis de Tocqueville remarked, "[s]carcely any political question arises in the United States which [is] not resolved, sooner or later, into a judicial question" (Tocqueville, 1994:280). In his observations on American democracy, Tocqueville examines, among other things, how the law can assist in preventing majority tyranny. Over 160 years later, do his words still ring true?

Nowhere has the concern about democracy and the rule of law taken on greater importance than in two areas that have captured wide media attention in the last decade: 1) the debate surrounding jury awards and tort reform and 2) the selection of judges for the federal and the state benches. This chapter addresses both of these issues and the arguments that have led proponents and opponents to categorically different policy recommendations about the appropriate solutions.

Agenda Issue One:
Jury Awards and Tort Reform

The U.S. system relies on two types of remedy against persons who are found to be in violation of the law. First, a *remedy at equity* requires specific performance, meaning that the individual judged guilty must carry out some specific act to fulfill her legal obligation. This can be a rather onerous task that requires court supervision to ensure that the defendant complies. Second, and the easier remedy to render, is the provision of a *remedy at law*. Under this, the defendant is required to pay damages (monetary compensation) to fulfill the legal obligation.

A tort is a civil wrong that is actionable in a court of law. Under tort law, you can sue someone for the personal injury that he or she caused you and receive damage awards to compensate you for your economic and emotional loss. The court may also award punitive damages to send a signal that such civil wrongs will be punished. Both of these damages appeared at common law (the law we inherited from England). Common law is the body of law that is decided on a case-by-case basis by courts within a country. It is judge-made law.

In recent years, the controversy over outrageous jury awards (both compensatory and punitive) has been the subject of political campaigns and battles in the state and federal legislatures. Much of the disagreement stems from the debate about the propriety of allowing damages that seem disproportionate to the allegations advanced by the plaintiffs. Most of us know the headlines of the more popular cases. Table 1. below illustrates some of the high profile disputes in 2002.

Table 1: Jury Awards

2002 Jury verdicts				
State	**Plaintiff**	**Defendant**	**Amount**	**For**
California	Dying smoker	Tobacco company	$28 billion	Cancer
Kentucky	Burn victim	Gas company	$271 million	Injuries
Michigan	Deceased's family	Ford Motor	$290 million	SUV crash
Texas	State of Alabama	Exxon Mobil	$3.5 billion	Oil royalties
Texas	Four-car accident	Cooper Tire Co.	$10 million	Car Rollover

Doctors Out of Control?

Advocates for allowing unlimited jury awards argue that this is the only way that grass-roots interest groups, consumer associations, and labor unions can challenge large businesses and corporations in the courts. They point to the fact that the number of tort suits filed in state and federal courts remained about the same between 1975 and 1990 and that within the last decade, the numbers have actually declined. Of the 10 million civil actions filed every year in state courts, only 10 percent are tort suits (half of these are auto accidents, 10 percent are medical malpractice, 3 percent are product liability, and the remainder concern a variety of legal issues) (Budiansky, et al., 1992, 1995).

Personal injury and medical malpractice have been at the heart of an ongoing legislative battle pitting the American Medical Association against plaintiffs' attorneys. Doctors working with a cohesive medical lobby argue that trial attorneys are litigating needlessly and are looking to get rich quick. Vocal and well-organized trial attorneys argue that the reason why there are so many lawsuits is that medical malpractice is so common.

While the number of tort lawsuits has declined in the last few years, the number of formal complaints to the Texas State Board of Medical Examiners (responsible for overseeing medical investigations) has doubled since 1996. In 2002, there were approximately 4,600 complaints against the 38,000 licensed physicians (and approximately half of the licensed physicians have some sort of malpractice suit pending against them by at least one person). The Board only investigated approximately 1,500 of the complaints, dismissing the rest as being outside the organization's jurisdiction. Of those remaining investigations, less than 10% resulted in disciplinary action—the rest were dismissed as "without merit." Ten doctors were required to turn over their licenses, but three were allowed to continue to practice on probation. Critics argue that the only recourse a victim has is the judicial system because professional boards will not adequately regulate malpractice. They highlight one of the more infamous cases of a Dallas spinal doctor who admitted he was a cocaine addict; he had multiple complaints...as well as fifteen malpractice suits. It took the board 12 years to revoke his license. This is part of the explanation for why Public Citizen's Health Research Group

(a non-partisan watchdog group) in 2002 ranked Texas 38th of the 50 states and District of Columbia for taking serious disciplinary action against doctors (*Houston Chronicle,* 2003).

Trial Attorneys Out of Control?

In contrast, tort reform proponents argue that such lawsuits are destroying our legal system because of frivolous lawsuits and extended, expensive litigation. Opponents of high damage awards argue that such litigation serves only to line the pockets of plaintiffs' attorneys who take advantage of victims' pain and suffering for their own business interests. In turn, high damage awards inflate the costs of doing business because such awards increase the risk of litigation and insurance premiums. Moreover, they argue that the system encourages the taking of "quick kill" cases because attorneys are more likely to take cases that are going to guarantee a return profit swiftly. This leaves other persons who deserve legal representation to pay the costs associated with hiring an attorney.

In Texas, Governor Rick Perry introduced legislation to limit punitive damages awarded to the victims of malpractice and to regulate attorney fees. This is in direct response to rising costs of malpractice insurance that is driving doctors out of business. Supporters of reform point to examples of hospitals closing their doors after decades of business. Examples abound everywhere of doctors being put out of existence, and Texas is no exception.

In 2002, approximately six to seven hospitals specializing in obstetrics/gynecology were forced to close because of high liability costs. Obstetrics/gynecology as a medical specialty has one of the highest premium rates for malpractice insurance, and approximately 101 of Texas' 254 counties do not have a licensed obstetrician within the county. Over 32 percent of *all* Texas doctors considered curtailing services in some degree in 2002 (Hopper, 2002). Moreover, doctors have taken to holding protest rallies on government property to highlight the financial burden of malpractice insurance. In Spring 2003, more than 800 doctors protested in South Texas, pointing out that insurance premiums increased more than 200 percent from 1999-2003 alone (Texas Medical Association www.texmed.org). While one in four doctors was faced with a new lawsuit in 2000, over eighty percent of those cases were resolved without any damages being paid. Supporters of reform argue that attorneys are taking advantage of the medical profession, hoping to hit the jackpot from a jury. Even if they do not succeed in most of their cases, ultimately they may prevail on that *one* case (Richey, 2002).

Are Contingent Fees and Punitive Awards the Problem?

Part of the reason why tort reform has been so criticized is because of the contingency fee and damage award system. Undoubtedly contingency fees have driven up the costs of insurance. Opponents of tort reform insist that the system of contingency fees, where payment is given only if the case is successful, allows "underdogs" to make "upper dogs" pay. In a contingency fee situation, there is a high risk but a high payoff. Plaintiffs' attorneys who bring these lawsuits on behalf of persons who would not otherwise be able to afford an attorney collect between one-third and one-half of the damage award in the event the lawsuit is successful.

In 1994, the American Bar Association reiterated its support for the century old practice of contingency fees that is in sharp contrast to our sister system of common law in Britain. Under English common law, such contracts are illegal, thus eliminating the kind of litigation we see in the United States in personal injury cases. It must be noted, however, that England has a legal aid system paid for by the government that allows persons to seek legal assistance in civil cases, so attorney costs are sharply reduced.

It is in the U.S. Supreme Court that the issue of excessive jury awards is ultimately decided. Prior to the 2002 term, the last time the Supreme Court decided a punitive damage award was in 1996. In that case, the High Court reversed a $2 million award to a man who purchased a BMW car that had minor body damage. By a 5-4 vote, the Court ruled that the award was excessive, even though the seller had refused to reveal that the car had been damaged and repaired prior to the sale. Justice Breyer, who authored the majority opinion in that case, argued that the criminal and regulatory laws provide a more equitable and routine manner of dealing with corporate wrongdoing that would both promote responsible behavior and the efficient allocation of resources to victims.

More recently, during the 2002 term, in *State Farm v. Campbell*, the U.S. Supreme Court considered whether a $145 million punitive damage award against State Farm Insurance was excessive (the jury only awarded $1 million for compensatory damages). The award went to a policyholder (Campbell) who was involved in a 1981 car accident. The company refused to settle a suit filed by other drivers because they thought the total amount due should be less than the $50,000 maximum coverage held by Campbell under the insurance policy. State Farm insisted that there be no settlement on the accident despite an internal report stating that the prospects for winning at trial were poor. At trial, the jury found against the company and the policyholder, and awarded the other drivers damages of $186,000. At that point, State Farm changed its strategy and said the company would pay damages only up to $50,000 and that the policyholder would have to pay the remainder. The insurance company's attorney told the policyholder, "You may want to put 'For Sale' signs on your property to get things moving." Eventually, State Farm did pay the full amount, but the policyholder sued, saying that the company should have settled the case and that he had been driven to the brink of bankruptcy for eighteen months because the company was trying to protect profits.

During oral arguments, the justices showed an unwillingness to make a determination about the appropriate ratio of compensatory to punitive damages. Such was also the reluctance of the Court in the 1996 case, but some thought the Court might be more willing in 2002 to send a clear signal about a reasonable standard for punitive awards. State Farm was concerned that, in this case, the punitive damages were 145 times more than the compensatory damages. Their argument was that such a jury award is clearly disproportionate to the harm suffered. Legal counsel for State Farm argued that a proportional award would have been one to two or three times the compensatory damages. Justice Souter clearly took issue with that, saying that any set number the court might determine could be seen as arbitrary and that juries were in a better position to decide such issues at trial. Depending on the outcome in the *State Farm* case, states may take subsequent actions through their legislatures to limit excessive punitive awards.

Agenda Issue Two:
The Selection of Judges
Federal Judges

As provided in Article III of the U.S. Constitution, federal judges are selected for lifetime tenure. They cannot be removed from office except by impeachment and conviction, and they cannot even have their salaries lowered while in office. Such measures were part of the Founding Fathers' desire to have judges act as neutral arbiters and to remain removed from the political process. As Alexander Hamilton noted in *Federalist #78*, the courts shall have "neither Force, nor Will, but merely judgment." Hamilton understood well that "independence of the judges is equally requisite to guard the constitution and the rights of individuals" from harm that might flow from "ill humours" by the "arts of designing men."

Despite this constitutional design to limit the politicization of the bench, over time, there have been numerous party battles regarding judicial appointments. In almost every legislative session both sides of the partisan aisle have accused the other of unprecedented attempts to "pack the court" with judges ideologically sympathetic to their party's cause. While most newcomers to judicial politics are usually surprised to find that there are political battles that go on behind the scenes of such appointments, the reality is that "court-packing" (putting your party's candidate on the bench) extends to the beginning of the nation's history. Indeed, the midnight appointments of *Marbury* v. *Madison* (1803) were nothing more than an attempt by the Adams administration to make a last grab at power. Chief Justice John Marshall, in his majority opinion establishing the power of judicial review, glosses over the fact that his *own* appointment to the High Court was part of the court-packing scheme that the Adams administration had used to try to get Marbury appointed. The only difference was that Marshall's appointment was accepted because his appointment (no surprise) had been secured successfully in time.

Battles over federal court appointments highlight the fact that the nominations of lower federal court judges have taken on a higher profile since the 1970s—as is also the case with U.S. Supreme Court Justices. This may be due in part to the growing media scrutiny that has captured the attention of the general public. Nonetheless, in virtually every Congress since the Carter administration, there have been record increases in the number of partisan battles over judicial appointments. President Jimmy Carter pursued a policy of filling as many lower federal court positions with qualified women and minorities as possible. His policy goal was to place candidates on the bench who would support liberal social and economic policies. It set in motion a debate about the diversity and ideological composition of the entire federal judiciary.

The tension continued throughout the Reagan administration, in part due to Reagan's policy of examining judicial backgrounds to determine how the judge would vote on abortion and affirmative action. While many accused President Reagan of having a "litmus test" for nominating candidates, the White House expressly denied asking potential nominees how they might vote in certain types of cases. During the Reagan era, Democrats blocked a number of candidates including Jeff Sessions (who went on to serve as a U.S. senator from Alabama). Sessions' name never reached the full Senate for a vote. Clinton candidates faced the same opposition, and one Michigan state judge--Helene White--waited four years but was never called for a hearing. In all, there were almost 100 vacancies of the 852 judicial seats when Clinton left office, leaving the Bush White House to quickly move on confirmations.

While the Bush administration had hoped to fill the offices quickly, there were delays in the process, in part due to partisan rivalry. They were worsened by the events of September 11th that stalled work in the Congress. When the process did get going, federal judge confirmation hearings for Bush candidates during the 2002-2003 session produced particularly acrimonious debate in the Senate Judiciary Committee. Democrats, who felt that Republicans had unfairly blocked Clinton nominees during the waning days of that administration, became increasingly hostile about a few key candidates. Republicans charged that Democrats were attempting a "pay back," unfairly blocking otherwise qualified candidates.

Two case studies illustrate the recent battle over the nomination of judges to the federal bench---Miguel Estrada and Priscilla Owen. President Bush first nominated Miguel Estrada in May 2001 to the U.S. Court of Appeals for the District of Columbia Circuit. Priscilla Owen was nominated in 2002 to the Fifth Circuit Court of

Appeals in New Orleans, Louisiana. The U.S. Senate blocked both candidates with parties on both sides accusing the other of partisan unfairness.

Miguel Estrada, just 39 years old, had been in law practice for less than 10 years. It was not his age, however, that angered Senate Democrats--it was his refusal to answer questions about his judicial philosophy. As a Honduran immigrant who graduated in the top of his classes at both Columbia University and Harvard Law School, the one-time clerk for Justice Anthony Kennedy and assistant in the U.S. Solicitor General's office looked like a guaranteed confirmation. Ultimately, the Democrats were successful in filibustering Estrada's nomination the first time around because of concerns that he would be conservative on abortion rights, affirmative action, and religious freedom. Estrada was criticized for declining to give an example of a Supreme Court opinion with which he disagreed, and he also refused to name one judge he admired until much later—submitting that only in writing. These are all questions asked by predecessors in three different administrations from Reagan through Clinton, but Estrada's steadfast refusal to answer them left Democrats arguing that he was an unknown quantity, leaving him vulnerable to a Senate filibuster. Even though Estrada had enough votes to be confirmed, Senate rules require a three-fifths vote (or 60 of the senators) to invoke cloture, which ends a filibuster and closes debate. Since Estrada did not have 60 votes, the Senate could not get to the point of taking a vote on his nomination.

The issue of donations to judicial campaigns from attorneys or special interests is not relevant at the federal level, but it came back to haunt state Justice Priscilla Owen (47-year-old Baylor law school graduate) when she was nominated to the U.S. Fifth Circuit Court of Appeals in 2002. Justice Owen sat on one of the state's two highest courts from 1994 to 2001 (the Texas Supreme Court hears all civil cases while the Texas Court of Criminal Appeals hears only cases arising from the criminal courts—see below). When Owens's name was put forward by President George Bush, opposition groups criticized her for taking money from attorneys and other interest groups who later appeared before the Texas Supreme Court. Of particular concern was her relationship with the Houston firm Enron. From 1993 until Enron declared bankruptcy amid scandal in 2001, Enron was the largest donor to Texas Supreme Court races (providing almost $135,000, according to Texans for Public Justice www.tpj.org). Owen alone was the beneficiary of $8,600 from Enron in her 1994 race. (No one ran against her in the 2000 election). In 1995, Enron asked the nine justices on the Texas Supreme Court to rule in its favor regarding taxes on its inventory. The victory for Enron resulted in a savings of over $225,000 in property tax assessments. While the U.S. Senate Judiciary Committee was concerned about impropriety during the hearings, ultimately it found that Owen followed the state's fund-raising rules. Like the nomination of Estrada, Owen's 2002 nomination failed for numerous reasons, including ideology. However, President Bush re-nominated Owen in 2003, and this time around, she received support from the Senate Judiciary Committee (which had a Republican majority after the 2002 election). When her name was forwarded to the full Senate, Democrats once again threatened to filibuster. However, in May, 2005, a deal was made in the Senate to bring judicial nominees to the floor for a vote and Priscilla Owen was confirmed for a seat on the Circuit Court.

State Judges

There are as many ways to choose state judges as there are states in the country. Variation in judicial selection processes is part of our unique structure of federalism that allows states self-governance. Options range from complete merit selection by the governor, legislature or nominating commission to the popular election of all judges at all levels by the voting population. Not all states have judicial elections. There are a number of different variations of state court selection processes and the number of terms

served. As Table 2 illustrates, Texas is unique among the states for partisan elections (all judges at all levels are chosen by partisan election). In contrast to the federal level where the president and the Senate play an important role, the most common method for initial judicial selection is by nominating commission set up under state law. Note also that the chart only lists states; it does not give an idea about the relative size of the state. Most of the larger states including California, New York, and Texas use some method other than nominating commissions.

Table 2.
Methods of Selecting State Judges

Merit Selection Through Nominating Commission*	Gubernatorial (G) Or Legislative (L) Appointment Without Nominating Commission	Partisan Election	Nonpartisan Election	Combined Merit Selection and Other Methods
Alaska	California (G)	Alabama	Arkansas	Arizona
Colorado	Maine (G)	Illinois	Georgia	Florida
Connecticut	New Jersey (G)	Louisiana	Idaho	Indiana
Delaware	Virginia (L)	Michigan	Kentucky	Kansas
District of Columbia	South Carolina (L)	Ohio	Minnesota	Missouri
Hawaii		Pennsylvania	Mississippi	New York
Iowa		Texas	Montana	Oklahoma
Maryland		West Virginia	Nevada	South Dakota
Massachusetts			North Carolina	Tennessee
Nebraska			North Dakota	
New Hampshire			Oregon	
New Mexico			Washington	
Rhode Island			Wisconsin	
Utah				
Vermont				
Wyoming				

* The following states use merit plans only to fill midterm vacancies on some or all levels of the court: Alabama, Georgia, Idaho, Kentucky, Minnesota, Montana, Nevada, North Dakota, and Wisconsin

According to the American Judicature Society, which monitors judicial selection and the subsequent training of judges, about 87 percent of trial and appellate judges face some form of election (either *retention* or *contestable* election). In many cases, judges are first appointed by some government official or body (governor, legislature, nominating commission, or combination) and are then subject to election. The types of elections also vary. In a *retention election*, the judge runs unopposed based on her or his record. In a

contested election, the judge runs against other candidates—of course, these elections may either be partisan, with the judge's party listed on the ballot, or non-partisan.

There is a greater tendency to allow contestable elections at the trial rather than the appellate court level. About 53% of the approximately 1,243 appellate judges face contestable election (the remaining 34% face a retention election). In contrast, about 77.3% of the 8,489 trial court judges (in general jurisdiction courts) take part in contestable elections. It is important to note that, in many states, there is a process for mid-term judicial vacancies so the percentage of judges that are "subject to election" may be overstated. Most state-level processes for mid-term judicial vacancies allow some governmental entity (typically the governor) to appoint persons to vacancies. When the eventual "selection process" comes around, the candidate holding the office has an advantage.

Judicial Reform

Reform of judicial elections centers on concerns about judicial independence, and the idea that judicial appointments should not depend on partisan power. The Progressives at the turn of the 1900s began raising judicial neutrality concerns, and reforms included the nonpartisan election of judges. While electing judges allows the public to have a voice in judicial selection, the concern is that judges may become captive to special interests that appear before their courts.

As a direct response to concerns about partisan capture of the courts, the *Missouri Plan*, also known as *merit selection*, was developed in 1913. Some argue that one variation keeps the best of both worlds—both merit and popular approval. Under the plan, judges are initially appointed for a set number of years by some entity (governor, legislature, or nominating commission), and then, subsequent to having served in office, the judge may or may not have to face a retention election by the public (and judges' names, not their party, appear on the ballot). In 1940, Missouri was the first state to introduce such a proposal, and debates about judicial reform have centered on some aspect of the Missouri plan over the years.

Supporters of the Missouri plan argue that merit selection is necessary to insure fairness in the court system because popular election leaves judges having to be careful in their decision-making. Making an unpopular decision might subject them to extra scrutiny in the next election. Worse yet, proponents of the merit selection system argue that when judges are popularly elected, it leaves them vulnerable to wealthy lobbyists and business interests who may seek to exert some influence in a future legal dispute. As with everything in Texas, this debate has taken on gigantic proportions recently as judicial campaigns have become hot topics for legislative reform.

Texas: A Case Study

One unique component of the Texas court system is the bifurcated nature of the state's highest courts. All but two of the U.S. states (Texas and Oklahoma) have one *highest* Supreme Court. These courts are the courts of last resort in the states before a case is appealed to the U.S. Supreme Court. Each state has different names for its highest court, with the vast majority of the states naming it the "Supreme Court." In a few instances, such as New York, Maryland, and the District of Columbia, the highest court is named the "Court of Appeals." In Texas and Oklahoma, however, there are two high courts: the Supreme Court (which handles all civil cases) and the Court of Criminal Appeals (which handles all criminal cases).

There are three distinctive trends in Texas judicial politics that critics point to as troubling for any system of justice: partisan dominance; campaign finance abuse; and, related to both, buying justice. There has been much criticism of Texas judges because they are all elected by partisan ballot (the Governor makes interim appointments to vacancies if a judge steps down or dies in office). The first development that persons point to as disturbing in light of judicial elections is that of partisanship and campaign finance. During the 1990s, the Texas Supreme Court became Republican as did the attendant donors seeking to donate to winners. The last Democrat on the Texas Supreme Court bench left in 1998. This is symptomatic of a decade-long trend in Texas where voters opted for GOP candidates in all three institutions of Texas governance. Over time, the state's highest civil court has become more conservative and has sided increasingly with pro-business interests, favoring limitation of tort liability. More interestingly, the trend of electing conservatives has occurred at the same time that there has been a shift in campaign donations by trial attorneys. Traditionally, this group supported Democrats while defense attorneys opted to support Republicans. This trend began to change in the 2002 election when trial attorneys contributed substantially to Republicans.

Second, critics charge that campaign finance is out of control, with some candidates to the state's highest civil court raising and spending over $1 million to serve as a Supreme Court Justice. This is not a phenomenon exclusive to Texas, as the

Center for Responsive Politics reports about the 2002 election cycle. In fact, in 2002, records for judicial campaigns were broken all around the country.

- U.S. Chamber of Commerce--$7 million to attack judges in five states who did not support the group's business agenda.
- Ohio Chamber of Commerce--$3 million to stop a judge who overturned a tort reform law that big business supported
- Ohio trial lawyers and unions--about $1 million to support the judge who had struck down the law.
- Michigan--more than $15 million spent on three judicial races (10 years earlier such races cost approximately $100,000 each).

The 2002 elections highlight the problem with campaign finance. As you can see from Table 3 below, incumbents raised more than challengers, but even in the open seats, fund-raising was pivotal. Fundraising for the state Chief Justice race between Phillips and Baker was low because Phillips had been a leading advocate for reform and refused "fat cat" donations. Texas has the highest contribution limits of the eight states that have partisan elections. For the Supreme Court and Criminal Court of Appeals, the limit for expenditures is $2 million. Persons may give up to $5000 per election (that means that you can contribute up to $15,000 if you give to the primary, runoff, and general election). Plus, donors can spread that money over the state's 14 courts of appeal, as well as the urban trial courts (note that limits are dependent on population in the district). Moreover, law firms and their members can give up to $30,000 to these candidates for each election, and political action committees (PACs) can give up to $300,000 per candidate.

Table 3.
Texas Supreme Court War Chest Inventory on September 22, 2002

Place Party	Candidate	Total $ Raised	$ Raised Last 3 Months	$ Spent Last 3 Months	9/26 Cash On Hand	Top Donors to Candidates
CJ/R	Phillips [(i)]	$5,603	$500	$4,784	$15,023	Gov. Bush Committee
CJ/D	Baker	$3,357	$757	*$12,626	$628	Banker Doug Cameron
1/R	Schneider[(i)]	$800,526	$220,252	$319,609	$138,448	Vinson & Elkins
1/D	Yanez	$362,640	$117,380	$71,370	$79,733	Watts & Heard
2/R	Wainwright	$913,021	$213,426	$101,306	$257,804	Vinson & Elkins
2/D	Parsons	$247,143	$117,646	$43,459	$165,011	Nix Patterson & Roach
3/R	Jefferson [(i)]	$1,030,874	$122,416	$80,861	$289,608	Vinson & Elkins
3/D	Moody	$150,414	$59,349	$35,093	$13,658	Nix Patterson & Roach
4/D	Mirabal	$604,564	$289,232	$90,796	$328,711	Fleming & Associates
4/R	Smith	$18,440	$12,940	$10,131	$2,267	Louis Beecherl/Will Perry
	TOTALS:	$4,136,582	$1,153,898	$759,277	$1,290,891	

(i) = Incumbent. * $10,758 of this amount was from direct expenditures of Baker's personal funds.

Third, critics of campaign finance and judicial elections use Texas and Oklahoma as examples that attorneys and interested parties are trying to "buy" influence with judicial donations. One study in Texas found that 79 percent of the attorneys and 48 percent of judges indicated that campaign donations have a "fairly" or "very" significant impact on judicial decisions (Scherer, 2001). If there is a vested business interest at stake, attorneys and interested groups may be more likely to donate to judges who support their view.

The results from a 2001 study examining the 1994, 1996, and 1998 judicial elections to the Texas Supreme Court found a greater likelihood that the Court will hear one's case if one has given to a candidate's campaign.

The 10 justices who faced an election during the period studied raised $12.8 million. More than half of this money ($6.7 million) came from lawyers, law firms, and litigants who filed appeals with the court during the same period. The justices were four times more likely to accept an appeal filed by a campaign contributor than they were to accept an appeal filed by a non-contributor. The justices were 7.5 times more likely to accept petitions filed by contributors of at

least $100,000 than petitions filed by non-contributors; and the justices were 10 times more likely to accept petitions filed by contributors of more than $250,000 than petitions filed by non-contributors. http://www.tpj.org/press releases/paytoplay.html

Texas Supreme Court Chief Justice Tom Phillips has supported reform and promised to take action after the 78th legislative session (2003-2004), hoping that state legislators would do the right thing. The most common reform proposal is that merit selection should be put in place, at least for appellate judges. The governor could appoint judges from nominees suggested by non-partisan boards. After that, incumbent judges could face retention elections so that "bad" judges could be removed. This is a popular way to remove judges in other states as well, although it must be noted that, just as there are numerous ways to nominate a candidate to the state bench, there are many ways to remove them as well. Whether it is through subsequent election, or the re-nomination of a judge by the governor and legislature after filling out a term, the states use a variety of methods for determining whether a jurist stays on the bench.

PRO & CON
Should the Names and Pictures of Sex Offenders Be Posted On College and University Web Sites?

Cases or controversies that come to the U.S. Supreme Court may be controversial issues, and during the 2002 term, the High Court tackled one such high profile case. It is one that at first glance seems easy to resolve—can the name of a sex offender be posted on web sites? Between 1986 and 1993, approximately 25 states enacted sex offender notification laws. After the murder of seven-year-old Megan Kanka in New Jersey by convicted sex offender Jesse Timmendequas in 1994, "Megan's laws" began to appear in many states and at the federal level. Under revisions to the original laws, Congress has added provisions that require states to 1) release the names of sex offenders, 2) establish a database of registrants, and 3) require that persons on college campuses (whether for employment or education) must register. If states do not comply, they may forfeit up to 10 percent of their federal anti-crime funding.

The State of Texas web site for sex offenders is located off the Department of Public Safety page. http://www.txdps.state.tx.us. To access the page, go to "On-Line Services," and then click on the "Sex Offenders" tab.

YES, convicted sex offenders who are employed or who attend institutions of higher education should have their names and pictures posted on web sites. Persons who have been tried, convicted and found guilty do not have a right to privacy or some other protection of the laws, especially where the person is a sexual predator who is on a college campuses (as either an employee or student). Since the inception of California's system in 1946, state governments have enacted laws based on their interest in preventing future sexual offenses. The community has a right to know if there is a predator in the neighborhood, and the defendant--who has been found or pled guilty--has only a minimal intrusion into his or her life compared to the threat that he or she poses to the community.

Sex offenders harm vulnerable children, and they are more likely to be recidivists, so they deserve to be singled out. Texas Representative Sheila Jackson-Lee points out that 50,000 children in Texas are sexually abused or neglected, and some national estimates indicate that over 650,000 children are harmed every year. Estimates vary according to states, but one California study found the following: 30 percent of sex offenders commit another offense within the first year, and 62 percent of offenders return to prison within two years. In Texas, most of the 8,160 child molesters in prisons are repeat offenders. The purpose of registration is to prevent future attacks by such persons, who are likely to re-offend. It puts the community on notice that someone in their neighborhood is a threat. If even one child is protected from sexual abuse, the law serves a worthwhile purpose.

Posting information on a web site is nothing compared to some actions that could be much more intrusive. Indeed, perhaps Texas should go further and require active notification rather than the passive release of information that the public has to seek out. Only 32 of the of the 50 states post to public web sites, and in some states, you must visit a local law enforcement agency or call a toll-free number and pay for the release of such information. In Louisiana, defendants can be forced to wear special clothes or sandwich boards explaining their crimes. In Washington, prison officials go door-to-door in neighborhoods where a pedophile or rapist has been released. Finally, Oregon requires molesters to place a sign--a scarlet M--in their windows. Indeed, the threat of posting information is nothing compared to the chemical castration law that Texas passed in 1997 which applies to second-time pedophiles.

Government has a compelling interest in providing the public with information in order to protect communities that may be in danger as a result of the convicted defendant's presence. When balancing the extent to which the courts should allow the posting of such information, the courts should decide in favor of upholding such regulations because of the unique problem posed by sexual offenders. It is only appropriate that such deviants be required to register for periods ranging from 10 years to life. According to the Parents for Megan's Law group (www.parentsformeganslaw.com), approximately 24% of offenders is failing to comply with state registries. We need greater focus on providing adequate funding and tracking procedures by state agencies, including the courts. This should include *more* stringent laws with more severe penalties for offenders who fail to comply.

NO, convicted sex offenders who are employed or who attend institutions of higher education should not have their names and pictures posted on web sites. The goal of protecting future victims from sexual predators is not adequately accomplished by publishing offender information. Politicians make symbolic gestures about stopping sex offenders while giving band-aid treatments to protect our children. Community notification violates the individual's privacy and due process rights, and it interferes with the defendant's rehabilitation. Someone may be trying to rebuild his or her life, start a new job, or go back to school. Instead, these persons will be harassed while state authorities mismanage information about dangerous predators. Law enforcement cannot keep up with dangerous persons who have registered, and college campuses will have a false sense of security about safety and will have to deal with misguided vigilante justice.

Politicians misrepresent the purpose of Megan's laws because of good publicity, and they do nothing to protect us. Strangers commit only three percent of sex abuse cases and six percent of child murders. Of the almost 650,000 children that are subject to abuse, neglect, kidnapping, or murder every year, about 95% will be harmed by someone who knows them --- not a stranger who is an unfamiliar face on an Internet site. Persons are 20 times more likely to be abused by a family member, a neighbor, or someone that the family *allows* close contact with the victim. Posting the names of sex offenders will not stop this abuse, and some states (like Connecticut) even allow judges to grant exemptions for community notification if the abuser is a family member. Studies about recidivist rates for sex offenders are controversial. In fact, part of the reason recidivism rates are so high is that a majority of offenders are re-incarcerated for not following registration guidelines. At least one study by the American Psychological Association indicates that the rates are actually much lower than other types of crimes (about 13%, compared to 40% for the overall rates of recidivism).

It is impossible to maintain the dissemination of information, and predators can easily avoid reporting. In one survey, at least 18 states, including Texas, were unable to provide *any* information about how many sex offenders had failed to register, and of the information available for the remaining 32 states, approximately 77,000 offenders were missing. One study in San Antonio, Texas, found that approximately 75% of the offender addresses was incorrect, and a California study estimates that about 33,000 offenders cannot be found anywhere!

Registration laws lull the public into a false sense of security, and the laws do not go far enough to protect us from violent behavior. For example, Scott Stoller (convicted child molester) left Seattle, Washington, and drove to Redmond, where there was no notification. He attacked two girls (ages five and six) whose parents assumed that their community was safe. Additionally, if states believe that notification is such a powerful tool, why is it that some states like California require you to dial a 900 number and pay $10 for information about two offenders? If having information posted is a deterrent, then why don't we post all information about everyone convicted of violent acts-including murder, attempted murder, or even driving under the influence where an injury resulted?

Persons who lawfully comply place themselves in fear of bodily harm. Posting public information interferes with the rehabilitation of the offender. If notification information is incorrect, innocent citizens can be attacked. In Dallas in 1999, a young Vietnamese man who lived at the address of a sex offender was viciously attacked and beaten unconscious. The four men yelled "child molester" and then left him for dead. Because there have been over 100 cases documented by authorities where innocent persons have been harmed as the result of inaccurate community notification procedures, the government is sponsoring vigilantism.

The Death Penalty

A difficult and controversial topic with which courts and judges must deal is the death penalty. The following information is from the web page of the Bureau of Justice Statistics of the Department of Justice (www.ojp.usdoj.gov).

- At the end of 2003, 37 States and the Federal prison system held 3,374 persons who had been convicted and sentenced to death for the crime of murder.

- Of that number, 1,878 were white, 1,418 were African American, 29 were Native American, 35 were Asian, and the rest were categorized as unknown.

- Forty-seven women were on death row at the end of 2003.

- The youngest person under sentence of death was age 19. The oldest was 88. Overall, the average age at arrest was 28. Two percent of those on death row were age 17 or younger at the time of arrest, although the Supreme Court has since ruled that it is unconstitutional to execute persons who were not yet eighteen at the time they committed murder.

- In 2004, 59 persons were actually executed, six fewer than the 65 persons executed in 2003. Of those executed in 2003, 41 were white, 20 were Black, 3 were Hispanic, and one was Native American.

- The method of execution in 2003 was lethal injection in all except one instance, when electrocution was used.

- Most persons on death row have prior convictions. In fact, one in twelve has a previous conviction for homicide.

- In 2003, the following states carried out executions: Texas (24); Oklahoma (14): North Carolina (7); Alabama (3); Florida (3); Georgia (3); Ohio (3); Indiana (2); Missouri (2); Virginia (2); Arkansas (1). There was also one execution in the Federal system.

EXERCISE 10-1
Conducting Legal Research

Conducting legal research is very straightforward. This exercise will assist you in finding information from the electronic data source LEXIS/NEXIS, to which most colleges and universities have access. You should begin using the U.N.T. library server (www.library.unt.edu). It is available in any of the computer labs, and you will need your EUID to access it from home. Once you are at the "Library," click on "Electronic Resources," then on "L" (Abstract and Index Database), and finally on "LEXIS/NEXIS Academic." From there, follow the tabs according to the questions listed below. This can be a helpful resource for conducting research in your other classes as well.

Finding U.S. Supreme Court Case Law

1. Find the U.S. Supreme Court case dealing with the sex offenders decided in 2003. Click on "Legal Research," and "Find a case." Be sure to type one of the citations exactly as it is listed below (you need use only one citation). You may want to use the "Citation" format because the "name" search will produce hundreds of hits, as names are so common.

The citation is *Connecticut Department of Public Safety* v. *Doe*, 123 S. Ct. 1140; 155 L. Ed. 2d 164; 2003 U.S. LEXIS 1949; 71 U.S.L.W. 4182; 16 Fla. L. Weekly Fed. S 142.

   a. How many and who are the justices in the majority opinion? _____

   _____

   b. Who wrote the majority opinion? _____

   c. Were there any dissenting opinions? If yes, by whom? _____

Finding U.S. Lower Court Case Law

2. Find a federal district court case decided in Texas regarding sex offenders and community notification within the last five years. Choose "Federal Case," "District Court," and develop a search string that incorporates words relevant to the case.
Hint: try **sex! w/5 offen! w/25 community w/10 notif!**. Note: do not use quotes to surround the words—type the string exactly as it appears in bold. Note also, the "!" in the search acts as a wild card to search all variations such as "offender," "offending," "offense," etc. the "w/5" string says "find all phrases where the word "sex!" appears *within 5 words* of "offen!" and that phrase appears within *25 words* of the second phrase regarding "community" *within 10 words* "notif!"

   a. What is the name of the case? _____

   b. What is the citation? _____

   c. What district court decided the case? _____

   d. What judge wrote the opinion? _____

   e. Did the court decide in favor of the defendant? _____

Finding News Stories

3. Click on the "News" category, and click on the tab "Guided News Search." Under the "Select a News Category," choose "U.S. News." Be sure that in step 2, you click on "Texas News Sources" as the news source. Run the following search (note that your date limit is six months; you may want to expand this if you do not find enough articles).

Answer the following questions.

    a.   How many articles were there regarding sex offenders? _____

    b.   Choose one article and list its title and author. Author: _____

         Title: _____

    c.   Give a brief summary of the news article you choose. _____

         _____

         _____

Finding Scholarly Articles

Judges, attorneys, and legal scholars author research publications about topical issues in law reviews run by law students and faculty from around the country and the world. These articles can provide topical and in-depth summaries of legal issues that are helpful for learning more about the work of the courts. Conduct the following research on law review articles.

4.   Click on the "Legal Research," then the "Law Reviews" and then the "Guided Search" tab. On the tab next to "Full Text," click and select "Title" as your area to search. Conduct the same search that you conducted above for the news story.

    a.   How many articles did you find for the last six months? _____

    b.   In the last year? _____ (you need to expand the date of your search to answer this question).

    c.   Find one article published within the last two years by Elizabeth Garfinkle (be sure to select the "Author" choice). What is the name of the article?

         _____

         _____

    d.   What is the law review citation where the article appears?

         _____

    e.   Give the author, title, and citation of an article within the last five years that discusses sex offenses and vigilantism (one search string would be in "Title" sex! w/2 offen! w/25 vigilant!).

         Author:_____Title:_____

         _____Citation:_____

Name		Seat	Score

EXERCISE 10-2
Learning About the Federal Courts

The U.S. Courts are now on the World Wide Web. Visit the official web site www.uscourts.gov/

PART I: Find the official web site for the U.S. Fifth Circuit Court of Appeals. Please answer the following questions.

1.   List the name of a recent opinion of a case and the citation to the case.

        _____

2.   What is the dispute about? _____

        _____

3.   What 3 judges heard the case (if it was an *en banc* panel, list all of the judges' names on a separate sheet).

        _____

4.   How many judges are listed under the "Judicial Biographies" category? _____

5.   How many judges are listed as permanently seated in New Orleans?_____

6.   In what other cities is court held?

        _____

PART II. Find the official web site for the District Court for the Northern District of Texas. Please answer the following questions.

1.   List the name of a "Notable Case." _____

2.   Provide the citation for the case and the date on which it was decided. _____

3.   What dispute was the case to settle?

        _____

        _____

4.   Choose one judge from the "Judicial Biographies" category.

        _____

5.   What president appointed that judge and on what date?

        _____

6.   Where did the judge attend law school?

        _____

7.   Examine all of the judges that are NOT senior or magistrate judges.

        a.   How many judges are there? _____
        b.   What is the partisan breakdown according to presidential appointments?
                _____Republicans   _____Democrats

Name		Seat	Score

EXERCISE 10-3
Finding Court Cases

Finding decisions of the U.S. Supreme Court has been made increasingly easier by advances in technology. Paper copies of court cases appear in four different citation formats, but the actual text of the cases is virtually identical no matter what the source, regardless of whether you find it in your public library or on the Internet. The material for both cases will be available at www.findlaw.com. Part of this exercise is learning how to find cases on public data sources. You can also find recent opinions on any number of web sites including supct.law.cornell.edu/supct.

PART I: Finding Cases by Name: On FINDLAW, go to "Legal Professionals", then "Federal Law", then "U.S. Supreme Court" click on the link. Under the "Party Name" search, find a case with the following name: State Farm v. Campbell.

1. _____ What is the citation to the case and year it was decided?

2. What was the High Court's decision about whether the punitive damages were excessive?

   _____

3. _____ Who wrote the majority opinion?

4. _____ Who wrote the dissenting opinion?

PART II. On FINDLAW, find a case that deals with cross burning and a Virginia law decided in 2003 involving a man named Elton Black (Hint: you may want to search through the 2003 cases. Use your search tool to find either name. You may also try doing a full text search using the word "AND" to connect terms you are searching for in the case).

1. _____ What date was the case decided?

2. What was defendant Elton Black accused of doing?

   _____

3. _____ Find a case decided during 2003 that involved the Connecticut

   Department of Public Safety and a sex offender (John Doe) and the application of Megan's law.

4. _____ What U.S. Circuit Court of Appeal delivered the lower court

   opinion?

5. _____ What justice delivered the opinion of the court?

6. _____ What justice submitted a "concurring in judgment" opinion?

Name		Seat	Score

EXERCISE 10-4
Profiles of Federal Judges

The demographics of appointed judges have changed over time (both at the Court of Appeals and the District Court levels), as the following table illustrates. Information about federal judges appointed throughout the court's history can be located online at the Federal Judicial Center http://air.fjc.gov/. You can also find the web site by searching www.google.com and entering the following search string in quotes: "judges of the united states courts." Once you go to the website, complete the table below by clicking on Federal Judges Biographical Database (http://air.fjc.gov/history/judges_frm.html).

Average age of Candidate	President Appointing Candidate
52.9	Franklin D. Roosevelt (FDR)
55.1	Harry S Truman (HST)
55.9	Dwight D. Eisenhower (DDE)
52.7	John F. Kennedy (JFK)/Lyndon B. Johnson (LBJ)
53.4	Richard M. Nixon (RMN)/Gerald R. Ford (GRF)
51.8	Jimmy E. Carter (JEC)
50.0	Ronald W. Reagan (RWR)
48.7	George H.W. Bush (GHB)
51.2	William J. Clinton (WJC)
50.5	George W. Bush *(107th Congress)* (GWB)
50.1	George W. Bush *(108th Congress)* (GWB)

Source: Sheldon Goldman. 1997. *Picking Federal Judges: Lower Court Selection from Roosevelt through Reagan.* New Haven, CT: Yale University Press. update www.fjc.gov

1. Construct your own chart below regarding demographics of judges for each president listed.

President	Total Judges Appointed	# Of White Males	# Of African American Women	# Of Hispanic Males	# Of African American Males
F. Roosevelt					
Truman					
Eisenhower					
Kennedy/Johnson					
Nixon/Ford					
Carter					
Reagan					
G. Bush					
Clinton					
G.W.Bush					

2.   How many judges left the bench because of death? _____

3.   How many judges left the bench by resigning? _____

4.   How many justices (judges) have served on:

   a._____ the U.S. Supreme Court

   b. _____ the U.S. Courts of Appeal

   c. _____ U.S. District Courts

   d. _____ Fifth Circuit Court of Appeals

   e. _____ U.S. District Court for the Northern District of Texas

   f. _____ U.S. District Court for the Eastern District of Texas

5.   How many judges have been Native American? _____Asian American? _____

6.   How many U.S. District Court judges were appointed by:

   a. _____ George Washington   d. _____ Ronald Reagan

   b. _____ Abraham Lincoln   e. _____ George H. Bush

   c. _____ Gerald Ford

7.   How many U.S. Supreme Court justices were appointed by:

   a. _____ Thomas Jefferson   d. _____ Jimmy Carter

   b. _____ James Madison   e. _____ William Clinton

   c. _____ Franklin D. Roosevelt

Name		Seat	Score

EXERCISE 10-5
Review of Key Concepts

Answer each of the following questions regarding the concepts in the chapter. Be sure to select the best answer.

1. _____ Which of the following is correct about the *remedy at law?*
   A. It allows courts to order defendants found guilty to perform specific activities as part of the judgment.
   B. It allows courts to order defendants to pay compensatory and punitive damages.
   C. It requires the plaintiffs to pay all attorneys' fees whether they win or lose.
   D. It requires that attorneys perform specific activities as part of the judgment if the lawsuit is found to be frivolous litigation.

2. _____ Which of the following is correct about *common law?*
   A. It is the body of law decided on a case-by-case basis that develops the legal rules governing a society.
   B. It is the system of legal aid attorneys that assist the general citizenry with bringing lawsuits.
   C. England has the same process of deciding personal injury cases that we do here in the United States because our common law is the same.
   D. U.S. juries are favorably disposed to giving plaintiffs jackpot jury awards because it wants to reward the common man.

3. _____ In the past 25 years, tort cases have:
   A. increased by over 300%.
   B. decreased to the point where they form only a negligible part of lawsuits.
   C. have increased about as fast as federal judgeships have been filled.
   D. have remained about the same, with slightly fewer cases filed in the last decade.

4. _____ Juries award _____for economic and emotional costs and give _____ to send a signal that such future illegal behavior will not be tolerated.
   A. remedy at law / remedy at equity
   B. compensatory damages / punitive damages
   C. remedy at equity / remedy at law
   D. punitive damages / compensatory damages

5. _____ What is one argument in favor of unlimited tort liability awards?
   A. Such awards allow "upper dogs" to sue "under dogs" for bringing frivolous lawsuits.
   B. The awards give the insurance industry a reason to require higher insurance premiums.
   C. Such awards help reward doctors who are not accused of medical malpractice to keep costs high.
   D. It requires that large businesses and corporations take responsibility for their negligent behavior.

151

6. _____ What is one argument against the use of contingency fees?
   A. Such fees allow attorneys who represent grass-roots groups to bring lawsuits that might not otherwise be possible if the group had to pay attorney fees up front.
   B. Such fees allow large companies with considerable legal resources to bring lawsuits against individuals for their negligent behavior.
   C. Such fees allow attorneys to take cases with the hopes that there will be a high payoff.
   D. Such fees allow grass-roots groups to collect punitive awards from attorneys that do not win cases.

7. _____ Which of the following is *true* about tort reform?
   A. Governor Rick Perry does not support reforming the tort system because he was a trial attorney before taking office.
   B. The state of Texas has not experienced the same level of damage awards that other states have seen in recent years.
   C. Governor Rick Perry advocates limiting punitive damages and regulating attorney fees.
   D. The use of lawsuits to combat medical malpractice in Texas has helped keep insurance premiums low.

8. _____ Which of the following is *true* about the selection of federal judges?
   A. There have been very few partisan battles in the confirmation process since the Carter administration.
   B. After President Jimmy Carter left office, virtually all of the vacancies were filled by women and minorities.
   C. President Reagan did try to appoint ideological candidates to the federal bench, and therefore he was not very successful.
   D. President Clinton was unsuccessful in being able to fill all the vacancies on the federal bench by the end of his term.

9. _____ Which of the following is *false* about the selection of judges to the state benches?
   A. The popular election of judges is used only by a handful of states with small populations.
   B. A number of states rely on nominating commissions to select judges.
   C. Justice Tom Phillips of the Texas Supreme Court is leading the call for reform in the way Texas selects judges.
   D. A majority percentage of trial and appellate judges is elected in some form of nonpartisan or contestable election either to gain the seat or after appointment by a statewide governmental institution.

10. _____ Which of the following is *false* about the removal of judges?
   A. Judges in the state of Texas are selected by a nominating commission and then must face a retention election.
   B. Federal judges can only be removed by impeachment and conviction.
   C. State judicial systems use a variety of methods for the removal of judges.
   D. Federal judges are given lifetime tenure and hold their office during good behavior.

Name		Seat	Score

EXERCISE 10-6
Summary of Key Principles

1. What is the difference between a *remedy at equity* and a *remedy at law*?

   _____

   _____

2. What is the difference between *compensatory* and *punitive* damages?

   _____

   _____

3. Give three arguments in favor of tort reform.

   a. _____

   _____

   _____

   b. _____

   _____

   c. _____

   _____

4. Why do attorneys take fees on a contingent basis?

   _____

   _____

5. What is the Missouri plan for judicial selection?

   _____

   _____

   _____

6. How are federal judges selected?

   _____

7. Why is it argued that federal judges are "de-politicized?"

   _____

   _____

8. Who have plaintiffs' attorneys traditionally supported in judicial elections and how is that changing in Texas?

   _____

   _____

9.   Why were some persons opposed to the nomination of Miguel Estrada and Priscilla Owen to the Circuit Courts of Appeals?

_____

_____

_____

_____

10a.   _____   How many states have partisan elections to select judges?

10b.   _____   How many states have nominating elections to select judges?

10c.   _____   How many states have combined methods to select judges?

11.   _____   What percentage of appellate judges is elected in some form (contestable or retention)?

12.   Who is a leading proponent of judicial selection reform, and how much did he spend in his 2000 campaign to get re-elected to the Texas Supreme Court?

_____

13.   What is the current proposal to reform the Texas system for electing judges?

_____

_____

14.   What are three arguments for opposing the popular election of judges according to the material you just read?

a.   _____

b.   _____

c.   _____

15.   What is the concern about judges being elected in Texas and who is one of the leading proponents of election reform?

_____

_____

Name		Seat	Score

REFERENCES

Chapter I

Adams, Henry. 1946. *The Education of Henry Adams.* Boston: Houghton Mifflin Company.

Glendon, Mary Ann. 1991. *Rights Talk. The Impoverishment of Political Discourse.* New York: The Free Press.

Hobbes, Thomas. 1994. *Leviathan.* Ed. Edwin Curley. Indianapolis: Hackett Publishing.

The Portable Thomas Jefferson. 1975. Ed. Merrill D. Peterson. New York: Penguin Books.

Locke, John. 1983. *A Letter Concerning Toleration.* Ed. James H. Tully. Indianapolis: Hackett Publishing.

-----. *Two Treatises of Government.* 1988. Ed. Peter Laslett. Cambridge: Cambridge University Press.

Machiavelli, Niccolo. 1996. *Discourses on Livy.* Trans. Harvey C. Mansfield and Nathan Tarcov. Chicago: University of Chicago Press.

Madison, James, Alexander Hamilton, and John Jay. 1 997. *The Federalist Papers.* London: Penguin Books.

Mill, John Stuart. 1989. *On Liberty and Other Writings.* Ed. Stefan Collini. Cambridge: Cambridge University Press.

Montesquieu, Baron de. *The Spirit of the Laws.* 1989. Eds. Anne M. Cohler, Basia Carolyn Miller, and Harold Samuel Stone. Cambridge: Cambridge University Press.

Tocqueville, Alexis de. *Democracy in America.* 2000. Trans. Harvey C. Mansfield and Delba Winthrop. Chicago: University of Chicago Press.

Chapter II

No references.

Chapter III

Henkin, Louis. 1996. *Foreign Affairs and the US. Constitution.* (2ND ed.) Oxford: Clarendon Press.

Mattei, Ugo and Jeffrey Lena. 2001. "U.S. Jurisdiction Over Conflicts Arising Outside of the United States: Some Hegemonic Implications." *Hastings International and Comparative Law Review* 24:381-400.

Morgenthau, Hans J. 1973. *Politics Among Nations* (5th ed.). New York: Alfred A. Knopf.

Morrin, Douglas 5. 2000. "People Before Profits: Pursuing Corporate Accountability for Labor Rights Violations Abroad Through the Alien Tort Claims Act." *Boston College Third World Law Journal* 20:427-446.

Chapter IV

Biskupic, Joan. "Supreme Court Overturns Religious Freedom Statute." *Washington Post,* June 26, 1997. P. Al. Note: *Washington Post* can be accessed at http://www.washingtonpost.com.

O'Connor, Karen, and Larry Sabato. 1997. *American Government: Continuity and Change.* Boston: Allyn and Bacon.

Chapter V

American Civil Liberties Union web site. Retrieved at www.aclu.org on January 27, 2003.

American Civil Liberties Union. September 2003. "Attorney General John Ashcroft's Assault on Civil Liberties." Retrieved on April 17, 2005, at www.aclu.org

American Library Association. "The USA Patriot Act in the Library. Retrieved on April 18, 2005, at www.ALA.org

Amnesty International. "Death Penalty Q & A." Retrieved at www.amnestyusa.org on February 21, 2003.

Avalon Project. Yale Law School. Retrieved at www.yale.edu on February 15, 2003.

Balkin, Jack M. "USA Patriot Act: A Dreadful Act II." *Los Angeles Times.* February 13, 2003. Retrieved at www.commondreams.org on February 21, 2003.

Court Online. "Texas and the Death Penalty." Retrieved at www.courttv.com on February 21, 2003.

CBS News.com. May 15, 2002. "Big Brother Is Watching, Listening." Retrieved at www.cbsnews.com on January 28, 2003.

CNN.com/Education. January 10, 2003. Retrieved on January 10, 2003, at www.cnn.com.

Death Penalty Information Center. "History of the Death Penalty: Part I." Retrieved at www.deathpenaltyinfo.org on February 21, 2003.

Death Penalty Information Center. 2005. Retrieved on April 18, 2005, at www.deathpenaltyinfo.org

Department of Homeland Security. "Travel & Transportation." Retrieved on April 17, 2005, at www.governmentguide.com

Doyle, Charles. April 1 8, 2002. "The USA PATRIOT Act: A Sketch." Congressional Research Service. Retrieved at www.crs.gov on February 15, 2003.

Eggen, Dan. December *25,* 2002. "FBI Seeks Data on Foreign Students." Retrieved at www.washingtonpost.com on February *15,* 2003.

Graham, Mary. "The Information Wars." The Atlantic Online. September 22, 2002. Retrieved at www.theatlantic.com on February 15, 2003.

Harpers Magazine. "Department of Homeland Security." Retrieved on April 17, 2005, from www.Harpers.org

Hentoff, Nat. *The Village Voice,* retrieved at *www.villagevoice.com* on January 27, 2003.

Herman, Susan. "The USA PATRIOT Act and the U.S. Department of Justice: Losing Our Balances?" *Jurist Legal Intelligence.* Retrieved at http://jurist.law.pitt.edu on January 28, 2003.

Isikoff, Michael. February 3, 2003. "The FBI Says, Count the Mosques. " *Newsweek.* p 6.

Nash, Gary, Julie Roy Jeffrey, Allen F. Davis, Peter J. Frederick, John R. Howe, and Allan M. Winkler. 1986. *The American People: Creating A Nation and A Society.* New York: Harper & Row, Publishers.

National Coalition to Abolish the Death Penalty. "NCADP welcomes largest commutation of death sentences in modern U.S. history." Retrieved at www.neadp.org on February 21, 2003.

OMB Watcher. "Patriot Act II Also Limits the Public's Right-to-Know." Retrieved at www.ombwatch.org on February 21, 2003.

Palmer, A. Mitchell. "Between the Wars: Fears of Dissent." Retrieved at www.gmu.edu on February 15, 2003.

Schnabner, Dan. July 1, 2002. "Patriot Revolution?" ABC News.com. Retrieved on January 28, 2003 at www.ABCNEWS.com.

SEVIS.net. Retrieved at www.sevis.net on February 15, 2003.

Totenberg, Nina. March 2, 2005. "Supreme Court Ends Death Penalty for Juveniles." National Public Radio. Retrieved on April 18, 2005, at www.npr.org

Unger, Irwin. 1989. *These United States. The Questions of Our Past.* Vol. II. Englewood Cliffs, New Jersey: Prentice Hall.

U.S. Constitution. "Martial Law." Retrieved at www.usconstitution.net on February 1 5, 2003. Walfish, Daniel. November 15, 2002. *The Chronicle of Higher Education.* A40.

Chapter VI

Arnone, Michael. "Texas Falls Behind in Plan to Enroll More Minority Students." *The Chronicle of Higher Education.* January 17, 2003. A23.

Axtman, Kris. "Affirmative action, Texas style, stirs criticism." *Christian Science Monitor.* February 12, 2003. Retrieved at www.csmonitor.com on February 18, 2003.

Cable News Network. August 28, 2003. "Michigan remakes admissions policy." Retrieved on April 14 at www.cnn.com/education

CNN.org. February 17, 2003. "Former officers file brief supporting affirmative action."

Epstein, Lee, and Thomas Walker. 1995. *Constitutional Law for A Changing America.* Second ed. Washington, D.C.: CQ Press.

Harris, John F., and Kevin Merida. "On Affirmative Action, New Perspectives Strain Old Alliances." *Washington Post.* April 5, 1995. AOL. Retrieved at www.washingtonpost.com on February 13, 2003.

Lederman, Douglas, and Welch Suggs. *The Chronicle of Higher Education.* November 8, 2002. p. A3 8.

Lum, Lydia. 1997. "Difference of opinion about Hopwood." *Houston Chronicle.* March *25,* 1997. Retrieved at www.chron.com on January 30, 2003.

Milem, Jeffrey F. "Why Race Matters." *Academe.* Retrieved at www.aaup.org on January 30, 2003.

National Center for Fair Testing. Retrieved at www.fairtest.org on February 1 8, 2003.

One Florida. Retrieved at www.oneflorida.org on January 30, 2003.

Powers, Scott. January 29, 2003. 'One Florida' Example Could Affect Affirmative Action." Retrieved at www.oneflorida.org on January 30, 2003.

Pressley, Sue Anne. "Texas Campus Attracts Fewer Minorities." *Washington Post.* August 28, 1997. AOL. Retrieved at www.washingtonpost.com on February 13, 2003.

Schmidt, Peter, and Jeffrey Selingo. "A Supreme Court Showdown." *Chronicle of Higher Education.* December 13, 2002.

Springer. Ann. January 2005. "Update on Affirmative Action in Higher Education: A Current Legal Overview. American Association of University Professors. Retrieved on April 14, 2005 at www.aaup.org

Texas Higher Education Coordinating Board. July 2004. "Closing the Gaps by 2015: A Progress Report." Retrieved on April 16, 2005 at www.thecb.gov

Understanding Prejudice.org. "Ten Myths About Affirmative Action." Retrieved at www.UnderstandingPrejudice.org on January 29, 2003.

U.S. Civil Rights Commission. November 2002. "Beyond Percentage Plans: The Challenge of Equal Opportunity in Higher Education." Retrieved at www.usccr.gov on February 1 8, 2003.

Chapter VII

Dodd, L. C. 1993. "Congress and the Politics of Renewal: Redressing the Crisis of Legitimation." In *Congress Reconsidered* Eds. L.C. Dodd and B.I. Oppenheimer. Washington, D. C.: CQ Press.

----- 2001. "Re-Envisioning Congress: Theoretical Perspectives on Congressional Change." In *Congress Reconsidered* Eds. L.C. Dodd and B.I. Oppenheimer. Washington, DC: CQ Press.

Fiorina, M.P. 1989. *Congress. Keystone of the Washington Establishment.* New Haven: Yale University Press.

Hibbing, J.R., and J.T. Smith. 2001. "What the American Public Wants Congress to Be." In *Congress Reconsidered.* Eds. Lawrence C. Dodd and Bruce I. Oppenheimer. Washington, DC: CQ Press.

Huntington, Samuel P. 1973. "Congressional Responses to the Twentieth Century." In *Congress and America's Future.* Ed. David B. Truman. Englewood Cliffs, NJ: Prentice Hall.

Lowi, Theodore. 1998. "Forward: New Dimensions in Policy and Politics." In *Moral Controversies in American Politics. Cases in Social Regulatory Policy.* Eds. Raymond Tatalovich and Byron W. Daynes. Armonk, NY: M.E. Sharpe.

Mayhew, David R. 1974. *Congress: The Electoral Connection.* New Haven: Yale University Press.

Meier, Kenneth J. 2001. "Sex, Drugs, and Rock and Roll: A Theory of Morality Politics." In *The Public Clash of Private Values: The Politics of Morality Policy.* Ed. Christopher Z. Mooney. Chatham: Chatham House Publishers.

Mooney, Christopher Z. 2001. "The Public Clash of Private Values: The Politics of Morality Policy." In *The Public Clash of Private Values. The Politics of Morality Policy.* Ed. Christopher Z. Mooney. Chatham: Chatham House Publishers.

Smith, Kevin B. 2001. "Clean Thoughts and Dirty Minds: The Politics of Porn." In *The Public Clash of Private Values: The Politics of Morality Policy.* Ed. Christopher Z. Mooney. Chatham: Chatham House Publishers.
----- 1999. "Clean Thoughts and Dirty Minds: The Politics of Porn." *Policy Studies Journal* 27: 723-734.

Wuthnow, Robert. 1987. *Meaning and Moral Order: Explorations in Cultural Analysis.* Berkeley: University of California Press.

Chapter VIII

Fisher, Louis. 2000. *Congressional Abdication on War and Spending.* College Station: Texas A & M Press.

Madison, James, Alexander Hamilton and John Jay. 1787. *Federalist Papers.* http://memory.loc.gov/const/fed/fedpapers.html. Accessed February 26, 2003.

Nelson, Michael, Ed. 1999. *The Evolving Presidency.* Washington D.C.: Congressional Quarterly Press.

Milkis, Sidney M., and Michael Nelson. 2003 . *The American Presidency. Origins and Development 1 776-2002.* 4th Edition. Washington, D.C.: Congressional Quarterly Press.

Pfiffner, James P., and Roger Davidson, eds. 2003. *Understanding the Presidency.* 3rd Edition. New York: Longman.

Roosevelt, Theodore. 1913. *The Autobiography of Theodore Roosevelt.* Centennial Edition. New York: Charles Scribner's Sons.

Spitzer, Robert J. 1993. *President & Congress. Executive Hegemony at the Crossroads of American Government.* New York: McGraw-Hill.

Taft, William Howard. 1916. *Our Chief Magistrate and His Powers.* New York: Columbia University Press.

Wilson, Woodrow. 1908. *Constitutional Government.* New York: Columbia University Press.

Chapter IX

McCubbins, Mathew, Roger Noll, and Barry Weingast. 1987. "Administrative Procedures as Instruments for Political Control." *Journal of Law, Economics, and Organization* 3, 243-277.

Stigler, George. 1971. "The Theory of Economic Regulation." *Bell Journal of Economics* 2, 3-21.

Chapter X

American Bar Association. 1998. *Recommendations of the Task Force on Lawyers' Political Contributions. Part II (Appendix II).* (Chicago, IL: American Bar Association).

Bell, Daryl. 2001. "Sex offenders Web Site Flawed: Violators' Addresses are Incorrect." *San Antonio Express-News,* May 7, 2001, p. B1.

Budianasky, Stephen, et al. 1995. "How Lawyers Abuse the Law," *US. News & World Report,* Jan. 30, 1995, pp. 50-52.

Budianasky, Stephen. 1992. "Order in the Tort," *Economist* (Survey of the Legal Profession), July 18, 1992, pp. 8-12.

Eyssen, Alex B. 2001. "Comment: Does Community Notification for Sex Offenders Violate the Eighth Amendment's Prohibition Against Cruel and Unusual Punishment? A Focus on Vigilantism Resulting from Megan's Law." *St. Mary's Law Journal* 33:101-142.

Garfinkle, Elizabeth. 2003. "Comment: Coming of Age in America: The Misapplication of Sex-Offender Registration and Community-Notification Laws to Juveniles," *California Law Review* 91:163-208.

Hanson, R. Karl, and Monique T. Bussiere. 1998. "Predicting Relapse: A Meta-Analysis of Sexual Offender Recidivism Rates," *Journal of Consulting and Clinical Psychology* 66:348-3 58.

Hopper, Leigh. 2002. "Hospital takes permanent maternity leave; High costs force obstetrics unit to close." *Houston Chronicle,* October 12, 2002, p. 1.

Houston Chronicle (Staff Writer). 2003. "Bad Medicine: Doctors' Malpractice at heart of Insurance Crisis." January 12, 2003, p. 2.

Inselbuch, Elihu. 2001. "Complex Litigation at the Millennium: Contingent Fees and Tort Reform: A Reassessment and Reality Check." *Law and Contemporary Problems 64:* 175-195.

Richey, Warren. 2002. "Court Weighs Limits on 'Jackpot' Jury Awards." *Christian Science Monitor.* Dec. 10, 2002, p. 2.

Scherer, Michael. 2001. *Newsletter: State Lines.* "Is Justice Undermined by Campaign Contributions?" Center for Responsive Politics: Washington, D.C. vol. III, No. 3 (published on-line www.opensecrets.org).

Tocqueville, Alexis de. 1994. *Democracy in America.* New York: Knopf, Inc.

U.S. Department of Justice, Bureau of Justice Statistics. "Capital Punishment Statistics." Retrieved at www.ojp.usdoj.gov on June 23, 2003.

Zielbauer, Paul. 2000. "Posting of Sex Offender Registries on Web Sets Off Both Praise and Criticism." *The New York Times,* May 2, 2000, p. B1.